I0145500

The Art of Living

Letters to my Children

By

Terry Lutes

Eliade Press

1

ISBN 978-0-615-30772-5

First Edition

Never be afraid
to tell truth to power.

Terry Lutes has led many varied and separate working lives:

- as a Counterintelligence Coordinator at an American Embassy

- as a paid political operative on numerous campaigns for the legislature, for statewide office, and for three presidential campaigns

- as a college professor of Political Science

- as a computer programmer and electoral database strategist

- as an economic research analyst and lobbyist for a trade association

- as an IT Manager, CIO and Solution Architect for 6 different government agencies

- as a Chief Fiscal Officer for a government agency

...and at present as the Chief Operating Officer for a government agency involved in economic development.

Books by Terry Lutes

- ❖ *Political Campaign Management, Strategy & Techniques*

- ❖ *Voting Behavior, 1968-1980*

- ❖ *Rural Political Behavior*

- ❖ *Political and Civic Socialization of Children*

- ❖ *Political Campaign Finance*

Preface

One day I woke up and I was 60 years old. I looked at myself in the mirror and wondered how I got to be this age. The easy answer is that I didn't die.

I have thus far lived a full and rich life.

Along the way I managed to raise two very bright and engaging children of whom I am extremely proud.

I can clearly see both behind, and in front of me the landscape of life as it is. Behind me, I see the many pleasures and happiness that has filled my life, along with the occasional bumps and silliness that marks my passage.

This wisdom hits us all one day. It comes as a breeze that suddenly blows away the foggy mist of our everyday existence and suddenly you see clearly all around you. It is akin to the view that springs forward into your line of sight as you reach the top of a high hill and observe all around you the magnificent panorama.

Additionally, I had an epiphany moment that became a transformative occurrence in my life.

A little over a year ago, my viewpoint concerning what was important in life changed dramatically when

I found out that my two-month old granddaughter Madison had a liver ailment. She was given stark choices---an operation or death. Then eventually a 95% likelihood that if the operation were successful she would subsequently need a liver transplant. It was the moment when everything I had previously believed was important, became meaningless.

The birth of one's first grandchild is a momentous event. My blessed event unraveled quickly into a possible tragedy and it shook me to the core of my being. Among all the worry, fear, and heartache was the general feeling of helplessness in the face of the precariousness of life.

I changed that day.

Madison had surgery and was given a guarded forecast. It was assumed that even though her surgery was a success that she would eventually need a liver transplant. There was a lot of guarded optimism from the doctors.

Since her operation she has defied all the odds and the dire predictions. While still not completely out of the woods, she may have been one of the 1 out of 20 who not only will survive, but also may well lead a normal life.

Through it all baby Madison displayed a most unusual and almost gleeful disposition. To watch this child, who has the happiest face and manner that I or anyone else has ever seen, cheered us up in the hospital, and during her recovery and subsequent near-normal growth has been a wonder to observe.

My daughter's anguish was the hardest thing for me to handle through the ordeal. I silently vowed that I would never take another day or thing for granted and that I would concern myself only with things that truly mattered.

The second act in the transformation involves a matter of finances. I was currently eligible to retire at the end of this past year. This past fall, I have sat and watched my retirement nest egg slowly dissolve in the stock market meltdown of October 2008. My nest egg that I had built over 20 years was cut in half in about 20 days. The most interesting thing was that I was not concerned. My attitude is "so it goes..."

Madison is healthy and thriving, as is my daughter Jamie, and my son Brian. I have food in the house, a good job, a house with no mortgage and two cars that are paid for and I am comfortably serene.

Life will go on just fine even if my entire retirement portfolio would disappear into cyberspace-----which is where it really is. Little electronic numbers on a database correspond into money that is, or is not, available to me to use to acquire things.

I am content because I have all the things that truly matter in life and I have learned to view life as a panorama rather than as a close-up.

The panorama view of life requires a healthy, observatory attitude combined with a keen sense of self. It also requires sufficient humility in order to dampen your rampant egotism.

My life's work, even though it has manifested itself in various surface disciplines, has on a professional level always involved being a social voyeur. Figuring out what makes people tick and then figuring out how to get to them, motivate them, and/or satisfy them has been my profession.

If I achieve nothing else in my life, I want to impart the lessons I have learned to my beloved children, Jamie and Brian, and my granddaughters Madison and Abigail. If there are others that could benefit from these lessons learned and whatever small wisdoms I may have acquired, these letters are for you too.

The library shelves are full of enough books on grand moralizing and self-righteous visions and I hope that my book does not come across as another one. In the pages that follow are lessons as I see them that I fervently hope help guide my children and others that I care about. The chapters are littered with quotations from people in all walks of life that I have found inspirational, resonating and at times filled with wry humor. Among my favorites is this one:

> *Make yourself an honest man, and then you may be sure that there is **one less scoundrel in the world**.*
>
> *Thomas Carlyle*

A note to all is a caution that most of us will live simple lives, but many unusual adventures, close encounters, and walk-in parts into the panorama of history have been a part of my life. A friend once remarked to me that I have lived a "Forest Gump" life full of lucky encounters, and fortuitous turns of fate.

I have been blessed with being at the right place, at the right time, on so many occasions that it has almost become the norm for me.

In the pages to follow I want to pass on to my children whatever wisdom I may have acquired during my lifetime. This book represents my humble attempt to give you the lessons of my life, so that you can use them in your life.

Hopefully you will find something of value.

This book is full of very piercing quotes from a wide variety of people that I have collected over the years and taken to heart for their poignant guidance. The world contains a great treasury of wisdom that has been passed down to us for thousands of years. A lot of very wise people have proceeded us on this planet and their advice on how to conduct our lives is as suitable today as when first uttered, no matter how long ago, and no matter in what culture their teaching first appeared.

In a recent book by Maya Angelou, that gave me one of my inspirations for this book, the author gave this advice to her daughter:

> *You may not control all the events that happen to you, but you can decide not to be reduced by them. Try to be a rainbow in someone's cloud. Do not complain. Make every effort to change things you do not like. If you cannot make a change, change the way you have been thinking. You might find a new solution.*
>
> *Maya Angelou*

I have always put great value in a good quote, the kind you wish that you had been the first to say. Great quotes carry great impact and common sense using only a few words. I am sorry that they are not more sensitive to gender neutrality. Many of the quotes are from a time when it was common "man" rather than to people in general. It was the style at the time that the quote was first written down and I have left them intact in that manner.

A good quote often summarizes beautifully the important point or thought.

Among my many favorites:

Life is a succession of lessons, which must be lived to be understood.

Ralph Waldo Emerson

Being your father is one of the greatest honors I have ever known. I hope that my thoughts will add further to your understanding of how life works and what I believe you should do to lead a life that is full of meaning, purpose, and happiness.

Jamie and Brian; this book is for you.

Table of Contents

PREFACE 7

TABLE OF CONTENTS 15

INTRODUCTION 17

EMOTIONAL HEALTH 35

MENTAL HEALTH 59

SOCIAL HEALTH 75

VALUES HEALTH 97

PHYSICAL HEALTH 117

SPIRITUAL HEALTH 125

ECONOMIC HEALTH 135

CIVIC HEALTH 175

RECOMMENDED READING 181

Introduction

Be careful to leave your children well instructed rather than rich, for the hopes of the instructed are better than the wealth of the ignorant.

Epictetus

On Philosophy

We all have a general philosophy that guides our day-to-day existence. Most of us have internalized our philosophies into a loose set of guiding principles that we have usually inherited from our culture, our family, our community and our associations. Our philosophies are composites of the conflicting smorgasbord of influences that we encounter in our lives, from our youngest years in the home thru all of the contacts, living arrangements, educational experiences, social encounters, and myriad other influences that enter into our lives.

Few of us really think much about our philosophies of life and since they are composite, they often contain intellectual conflicts and inconsistencies. They also are subject to ongoing change as we age, encounter new experiences, learn new lessons of life, and encounter the rough and tumble of day-to-day living.

Your philosophy of life becomes your "mission statement". Emerson had one of the better ones I have read:

> *To laugh often and much; to win the respect of intelligent people and the affection of children; to earn the appreciation of honest critics and endure the betrayal of false friends; to appreciate beauty, to find the best in others; to leave the*

world a bit better, whether by a healthy child, a
garden patch or a redeemed social condition; to
know even one life has breathed easier because
you lived. This is to have succeeded.

Ralph Waldo Emerson

As a 17-year-old freshman in college, I was first introduced to various organized philosophies of life. This was in the mid-sixties, when many in my generation were being both allowed and encouraged to think on our own and to challenge our parent's dogmas and folkways.

While my peers were experimenting with various "new age" philosophies, I was introduced to an older philosophy, stoicism, and it was one that was to grab me and become the foundation of my life.

The book that first grabbed hold of me back then was ***The Meditations*** by Marcus Aurelius. His stoic philosophy spoke to me in a most profound way and it was a philosophy of life and an approach that I found that I had already adopted as my own, but reading about it gave foundation to my own internal belief and attitude system. I found that I was already a stoic, I just did not know it by an established body of belief and thought.

The stoic view of philosophy is not as an interesting pastime or even a particular body of knowledge, but is a way of life. Stoics define philosophy as a kind of practice or exercise in the expertise concerning what is beneficial. Stoicism teaches that once we come to know what we and the world around us are really like, and especially the nature of value, we will be utterly transformed. The *Meditations* of Marcus Aurelius gave me a fascinating picture of a would-be Stoic sage at work on himself. The book, also called *To Himself*, is the emperor's diary. In it, he not only reminds himself of the content of important Stoic teaching but also reproaches himself when he realizes that he has failed to incorporate this teaching into his life in some particular instance.

The Meditations taught me the inner freedom that we can experience when we step back into ourselves and listen to our mind. The cultivation of this inner freedom, says Marcus, is both our deepest human possibility and the real root of the self respect and moral power for which we yearn---the ability to love and act justly in the conduct of our lives.

Subsequent to my discovery of stoic philosophy, I began what would be a life-long learning and practicing effort at internalization of a coherent philosophical approach to living. I read most of the classical and contemporary stoic philosophers and developed my own unique composite set of beliefs and attitudes.

I further branched out in the development of my personal philosophical approach to life by the study of religions and mythology. I have always sought to understand the meaning of life and the purpose for existence. I have been fascinated with the motivations behind religion-like devotions. My travels have taken me to Mayan Temples, Buddhist Shrines, Pagan Circles, Hindu Centers, Cathedrals, and the myriad old rocks being worshiped in the Holy Land.

I have thus been a practicing stoic for over 40 years now. It has been my religion, my moral compass, and the motivational engine of my life.

In the 2nd Century AD, the lectures of the Roman stoic philosopher Epictetus were written down by his students and eventually became a book called the *Art of Living*, which is the same base title that I have chosen for these letters to my children. The students of Epictetus included the young Marcus Aurelius, who would become an Emperor of Rome. This book is a modest 21st century rendition of the type of instructions Epictetus put forth for his students so very long ago.

On Principles

We all talk about our "principles", but what do we mean by that?

My guiding principles have been based upon several old-fashioned words--------duty, honor, and dignity.

- I have a keen sense of duty and responsibility.

- I believe in doing the right thing whenever possible.

- I believe in maintaining my dignity no matter what happens.

- And always to conduct myself with honor and courage.

The following are my two favorite quotes about the subject:

The only thing necessary for the triumph of evil is for good men to do nothing.

Edmund Burke

To know what is right and not do it is the worst cowardice.

Confucius

Have I always lived up to my principles? Of course not. To be truly human is to be imperfect.

What counts is to always be trying---- to make a living, conduct yourself with others, raise a family, and generally make your way in this world by living your life according to some guiding principles as your continual intent.

Being true to your principles is not the perfection of results, but rather the intensity of the effort.

You will need to mentally articulate your own set of guiding principles. Do not expect them to be necessarily complete and thoroughly formed at an early stage.

Guiding principles help you reach important decisions about today and your future, listening to your heart and doing the right thing for yourself, and those you care about,

> *I skate to where the puck is going, not to where it's been.*
>
> *Wayne Gretzky*
>
> *The trouble with not having a goal is that you can spend your life running up and down the field and never scoring.*
>
> *Bill Copeland*

When a man does not know what harbor he is making for, no wind is the right wind.

Seneca

Celebrate what you've accomplished, but raise the bar a little higher each time you succeed.

Mia Hamm

The man who removes a mountain begins by carrying away small stones.

Chinese Proverb

Before we set our hearts too much upon anything let us examine how happy those are who already possess it.

Frances Rochfoucauld

Most of us do not really have goals in any sort of well-articulated way. We have to-do lists, we know things that we want, we are aware of our needs, we have mini plans to do some things but mainly we are just going with the daily flow of life.

The first thing to understand about goals is that they are not wishes. A wish is something vague that we want to have happen to us. A goal is something that we want to make happen. A goal is a clear achievement that we seek and work towards.

We get up in the morning, go through a set sequence

of morning get-ready-for-the-day functions, clothe ourselves, get in our car or hop on the public conveyance and go to work, school or some other activity. Then at that place we go to, we go through another set of often-sequenced functions. Mine goes like this: I park my car, walk to my office, unlock my door, turn on the lights, turn on my coffee pot, take some papers and files out of my briefcase, start my computer, and so it goes. Then other people begin arriving and we all engage in those morning social niceties.

Then I go to lunch.

I then go home.

In between it all, I do the work for which I am being paid.

The days turn into weeks. The weeks into months and the months into years.

This is going with the flow.

Goals are something different all together.

I often begin discussions with my staff during their annual evaluations by asking them a single question----what do you want to be doing in five years?

That question is usually met with silence.

Most people do not know where they want to be

in five years. They have mini-goals related to travel, purchasing more stuff, and family-related aspirations.

But goals? Rarely. Most of us are going with the flow.

Goals are stakes in the ground. Goals are things you want to achieve or attain by a general or specific point in the future. When you place these stakes in the ground, you can then make a plan on how to get from here, to there.

Once you have your stakes in the ground, the here and the there, you can then map out the intervening steps, or milestones, that will get you to your goals.

Plans do not have to be elaborate, just achievable. What is important is that you have identified what needs to be done to achieve your goals and have mapped out somewhat how you are going to get there.

But on one final note this quote:

> *We must be willing to get rid of the life we've planned so as to have the life that is waiting for us.*
>
> *Joseph Campbell*

When and if you don't achieve your goals the healthiest attitude to take is that you probably weren't supposed to get there. It just wasn't supposed to happen. Whether you want to attribute this to the will of God, or the result of fate doesn't matter.

No fault. No blame. No regrets.

Just move on.

On Priorities

Realize at all times that you will never have the time, the energy, the money or the patience to do everything that you think that you want to do on a given day, in a given week, in a given month or in a given year.

You need to learn how to prioritize and then to focus on what you can achieve in your ever-morphing set of priorities.

Some things will always be a higher priority like sleeping, eating, earning money and other basic needs. These are the things that you must do in order to be able to survive. They are priority #1 items.

Then there are the life housekeeping things that I will label as priority #2 items. These are the day-to-day activities like shopping, cleaning, grooming, paying bills, medical attention and other things you must do at some point. Not necessarily in the finite sense but things that you should do regularly. What is important is that these priority #2 items take time, energy and money. These are your diminishing resources for determining everything that you can achieve.

Then come the possible, or probable priorities. These, which I will call priority #3 items, are activities that we feel obligated to do like calling and visiting relatives, responding to your boss's special non-work requests, activities with friends and loved ones, civic or volunteer activities and general requests from others. Again, these all subtract time, energy and money from your total resource pool.

The final categories of priorities are the choice activities that I will call priority #4. These include watch TV, reading, going to movies, attending events, going on vacation----in other words everything else.

The main thing to always keep in mind is that most of the resources that determine what priority #4 activities that you can achieve are limited by what remains after you take care of #1-#3. Sure, you can cut back on sleep, not visit grandma, not stop to eat, but are you really going to do that?

Better to prioritize your use of your finite resources and probably more importantly decide what priority #4 activities to NOT do.

Not doing things is itself a decision. Things not done are your resource savings account----the place where you find the extra time, energy, and the money to do the things that you <u>really want to do!</u>

About 20 years ago I quit watching TV at night except for occasional news shows. Instead I read books and publications of all kinds and all genres. I feel better for my choices and I think I have led a richer and fuller life because of the decision, but I do not begrudge others who choose to do different things with their time and energy.

Freedom to choose is a blessing. The only advice I have to offer is to choose wisely and be happy with whatever it is you choose to do with your time, your energy, and your money.

On Rules

Every custom was once an eccentricity; every idea was once an absurdity

Holbrook Jackson

All truths began as blasphemies

George Bernard Shaw

Rules are necessary to control behavior, activity and the everyday functioning of civilization. Without rules, driving a car would be a demolition derby, building components would not fit together and function properly and society would be completely dysfunctional.

We all break "the rules" everyday, but we often know we are breaking them. It is all in the manner, the degree and the intent. For most of us, our rule breaking is minor.

It is an irony though that most progress and innovation often require the conscious breaking of rules. Challenges to rules are a rebellion, whether they occur in the workplace or in society in general. In the face of true tyranny, such rebellions are often necessary to bring about change.

On Health

Health is the key to happiness and the quality of your life. Most of us are generally born with good health. Lifestyle choices, behavior, heredity, and circumstance can alter the nature of your health at various points during your lifetime.

Health is not just physical health, although that is one of the most important. It is your mental health, emotional health, spiritual health, and economic health that determine your overall quality of life. Each type of health bleeds into the other type to form the general mosaic that determines your well being.

Good health is about discipline and actions.

Good health is about doing the right things and avoiding the wrong things.

Good health is about balance and attitude.

Good health is about taking control of your mind, your emotions, your spirituality, your attitudes and is about keeping your body in good condition for the journey of life.

For the most part, you control your health by your choices and actions. While external factors like disease and accidents can affect your health, the main factor affecting your overall health is you.

It takes hard work to stay healthy. It also takes knowledge, understanding and determination, but most importantly, it takes a proper attitude.

Emotional Health

Emotions are the engine that controls every facet of your life. Emotions determine how well we deal with the good and the bad, how we relate to others, and how they view and relate to us. It effects whether we engage in good behavior or bad behavior. The bottom line is that emotions can make us or break us.

It is all about attitude. I will come back to this word repeatedly because attitude is extremely important to determining your overall health.

Attitude in its most simplistic sense is about seeing the glass half-full and being happy, or seeing the glass half empty and being sad.

On Mindfulness

Being actively attentive or deliberately keeping something in mind is essential to attaining emotional control, focus and stability. The essence of being a human being is the ability to reason. We have the capacity to think through our actions before we take them, to think of consequences and alternatives. Yet having this capability does not automatically mean that we will. Going with the flow of life, being led by others, acting on impulse, and engaging in mindlessness is easier, often causes less friction, and does not create angst.

Mindfulness makes us pause before we speak unnecessarily, not eat when we are not hungry, or not take an unneeded action. Mindfulness, while akin to caution, is something a little more. It is the exercise of the human will and continual awareness.

Mindfulness must be obtained through determination, concentration and the focused application of attention. Certain exercises like Yoga and Tai Chi train the body and mind to be mindful, but we don't need to run out and buy a yoga manual and a mat to learn mindfulness.

It can come from within us.

If we tend to overeat we can concentrate on being mindful of everything we put in or mouth and stop ourselves from mindless eating. Mindless eating is why the open bag of chips at our side becomes the empty bag.

If we tend to blurt out things that are best left unsaid we can concentrate on mindful exercises like mentally counting to 3 seconds before we speak.

There is no magic bullet to mindfulness. It must come from within and we must do it for specific reasons and outcomes, or in the avoidance of unwanted outcomes.

Mindfulness is quite simply mental discipline and focus.

On Control

Recognizing when you're fighting reality spells the difference between guaranteed misery and a life filled with peace and contentment.

Richard Carlson

Happiness requires an acceptance of the fact that much of our daily existence, our circumstances, and what happens within our life are outside of our control. It is important for serenity that we not only accept what we cannot change, but that we give up trying to be in control.

Your ability to lead a tranquil life is dependent upon your ability to clearly distinguish between things you can control and things that you cannot control. Anguishing and worrying about things which are out of your ability to control gains you nothing but stress and can cause you fruitless anger.

You control your mind, your attitude, and your voluntary actions. All else is circumstance.

Things outside of your control are often determined by the actions of others or by the fates of nature. While you can try to influence what others do, you often cannot control them.

Circumstances

When something happens, the only thing in your power is your attitude toward it; you can either accept it or resent it.

Things and people are not what we wish them to be. They are what they are.

Epictetus

For peace of mind we should accept events as they happen. When you break your favorite object, it is broken. We cannot turn back the clock. While we can learn lessons from events, once they occur, they are done. Every event that occurs in our life that we didn't want to have happen confronts us with the issue of how we deal with it. We will often times in our life have to call upon our inner strength and resolve. These strengths are often submerged until called upon.

As time goes on and life knocks us about a bit we become better at dealing with circumstances. We learn to look beyond the incident itself, to learn another lesson, and to move on.

Acceptance

You must learn to accept the fact that the grass on your side of the hill is probably as green as it is ever going to be. While you should never cease to strive to make our lot in life and our circumstances better, you must never lose sight of the reality that what you have now may be about as good as it gets with only minor incremental improvements most likely to happen. If you spend too much time dwelling on what is wrong in our lives, rather than appreciating and accepting what you currently have you are liable to be continuously frustrated and discontented.

There are rewards for accepting your day-to-day life just the way it is. Your level of satisfaction will increase, and your level of contentment will be your reward for accepting that were you are at may just be as good as it gets. Enjoy it.

Acceptance is the ability to persevere through whatever life throws at you, acknowledge the event, take a deep breath, and then move on with the business of living.

Without acceptance you run the risk of becoming a victim for as long as our painful memories are kept alive and active.

Concerns

Concerning yourself with another's business, that does not effect you, those you care about, or issues you believe in, is a waste of energy and attention. Your attention is a limited resource. When you expend it on things, which are not your concern, you take away from things that do concern you.

On Choices

A person has three choices in life. You can swim against the tide and get exhausted, or you can tread water and let the tide sweep you away or you can swim with the tide, and let it take you where it wants you to go.

Diane Frolov

Life is a series of voluntary and involuntary choices that you all make consciously, unconsciously, or semi-consciously as you move through your years.

We often profess that we are independent thinkers making voluntary choices, for the most part; we do what is expected, what is acceptable, or that which we are conditioned to do. These holds true whether we have grown up and lived within a traditional protective family cocoon or have been seemingly free.

Many of us want to break free from the artificial constraints of our upbringing or our heritage.

Nevertheless, breaking free requires constant reminders, such as from the Bhagavad-Gita, which advises that "one must honor one's unique life predicament; one cannot imitate another's".

On the other hand, to quote another sage: "To one's

own self be true".

Everyone must pick and choose, borrow and morph, from all of life's teachings and guides, that which in combination uniquely fits the individual you. But, you must keep in mind that choices are mostly voluntary— the have-to's are in our head. There are the expected choices, the guided choices. There is very little anyone can do to make you make certain choices. Some things are important and they "should" be done, but they are still voluntary.

> *The greatest power that a person possesses is the power to choose.*
>
> *J. Martin Kohe*

While life is a series of choices that you make every hour, of every day, we don't always make the right choices. We all make mistakes, wish we could make some choices over again, and will always have some regrets and remorse for bad decisions.

There are no perfectly certain choices to make in every given circumstances----there are only the best choices we can make at the time we have to decide.

Make your choices, and once having made them, move on. Do not look back. Do not beat yourself up for making mistakes. Learn from your mistakes and remember them the next time, but don't dwell on them to the detriment of living for today.

On Passions

Absolutely nothing in this world has been accomplished without passion.

George Wilhelm Fredrich Hegel

A life with no passions is dull and lifeless. To have no passions is to have no soul. Whether it is sports or the arts, television sitcoms or live opera, most of us will have passions for some sort of activities, people, causes or hobbies.

It is in the nature of these passions, and whether they are negative or positive passions, that will reflect on how we affect those whom we are close to, whether it be family or friends.

Pleasures

It is the part of a wise man to resist pleasures, but of a foolish man to be slave to them.

Of pleasures those, which occur most rarely, give the greatest delight

Epictetus

Pleasures can be simple or elaborate, exorbitantly expensive or surprisingly affordable. Whatever makes you happy, so long as it does not come at the expense of others, or of your good name are probably OK.

I have always strived to take my pleasure in familiar and repeatable ways. An ice cream cone while sitting on a park bench on a hot day is the type of thing that comes readily to mind. Reading a good book that enlightens or entertains me is another. Gazing across an ancient work of art or architecture in a beautiful setting is yet another.

Pleasure is anything that pleases the senses and makes you feel alive, that fills you with awe, or leaves you in rapture at life.

On Journeys

> *Travel has a way of stretching the mind. The stretch comes not from travel's immediate rewards, the inevitable myriad new sights, smells and sounds, but with experiencing firsthand how others do differently what we believed to be the right and only way.*
>
> *Ralph Crawshaw*

One of those travel experiences that demonstrates this stretching of the mind involves learning about Tibetan funeral practices on a visit that I made to that land in 2005.

What I learned was that the people of Tibet did not bury their dead. Whether this was out of some religious or practical reason I never asked about for what they did do with their dead rather shocked my Western sensibilities.

They have two basic methods and I never learned if it was a choice or opportunity reason that made a family choose one method over the other.

The first method involved taking the deceased to a mountaintop and laying them out for the vultures to devour.

The second involved weighing them down with

rocks and dumping them ceremoniously into a river to be devoured by the fish.

My Tibetan guide told me that this return to nature was a basic part of the Tibetan Buddhist philosophy and that he thought that our Western way of burial to be both barbaric and ghoulish. He told me about seeing a European cemetery in Hong Kong and it made his skin crawl.

Travel to foreign lands will take you out of your cultural comfort zone, but only if you are willing and capable of stepping outside of your zone with an open mind.

Shortly after our Tibetan guide told us about the funeral practices we stopped at a riverside restaurant for lunch. None of us ate the fish or the large chicken-like offerings that the restaurant presented.

The advice that follows is more practical then philosophical but is the result from my own often hard-earned experience.

Destinations

Except for a few war-ravaged countries and failed-state countries there should be no destination that you should be afraid to journey to. While many areas of the world require more heightened cautions than others, the same can be said for many parts of America and especially in our big cities.

I have found that few parts of the world are as dangerous as the United States. We just don't think about the dangers in America as we do about those in some foreign places. Two of the places in the world that I have felt the safest were in Cairo in Egypt and Jerusalem in Israel, yet so many of my fellow Americans are petrified at the thought of visiting either country.

Most countries of the world simply do not have within their culture the person-to-person type of violent crime that we do in America. While many have the same petty theft problem that exists anywhere that tourists travel, most do not have the individual-based violence that we have in the United States.

Officials

When traveling, especially outside of the United States, do not be a pushy, boisterous and a typically ugly affluent Westerner when dealing with government officials. This especially holds true with those who can arbitrarily detain you during your travels like security, customs, and police officials.

You should be polite with them no matter what happens, listen attentively to any question they may ask, and respond respectfully to them.

In order to just make your way through the bureaucracy of entering and leaving a country you should try not to stand out in any way.

Packing

The best advice I ever heard about packing for a trip is that whenever you think you have everything laid out for your suitcase and wallet then:

> *Take half the clothes and twice the money that you intended to take.*

Light is always the best. I have traveled tens of thousands of miles literally around the world with untold pounds of stuff I never needed to take. We all usually take too much of "just in case" stuff.

Take clothes that you can wash out that will dry overnight and remember that you can buy clothes, often-local dress, while traveling. Also never take clothes, or anything else for that matter, that you would be bothered if you lost, or if you simply threw it away.

On Happiness

A sense of contentment is a key factor for attaining happiness

14th Dali Lama

Once we understand that the world won't devote itself to making us happy, we begin to accept that responsibility for ourselves.

Hal Urban

Happiness can only be found within yourself. This requires indifference to external conditions. Happiness cannot rely upon things you do not control, or on possessions, or on others.

Happiness is what we feel when things are going well, when we are getting what we want. It is the result of what is happening on the inside of our lives.

But always remember:

Even a happy life cannot be without a measure of darkness, and the word "happy" would lose its meaning if it were not balanced by sadness.

Carl Jung

Joy

There is no such thing as the pursuit of happiness, but there is the discovery of Joy.

Joyce Grenfell

Joy is a deep satisfaction with life. Joyful people are not just happy with life, they delight in small things, they are comfortable in their circumstances, and they see the positives in what they have in life.

Joy, rather than happiness is the goal of life, for joy is the emotion, which accompanies our fulfilling our natures as human beings.

Rollo May

Joy is the ultimate goal of being happy. It is waking every morning with a song in your heart, a spring in your step, and a smile on your face.

To live with joy is to live in rapture at being alive, firm in your prospects, confident in what every day will bring, and bountiful in your outlook on life.

On Fears

*I have not ceased being fearful, but I have ceased
to let fear control me. I have accepted fear as a
part of life----specifically fear of change and fear
of the unknown; and I have gone ahead despite
the pounding in the heart that says; turn back,
turn back, you'll die if you venture too far.*

Erica Jong

*We must constantly build dikes of courage to
hold back the flood of fear.*

Martin Luther King, Jr.

Many people have real and imagined fears. For
some people these fears can negatively affect their
ability to function and enjoy a happy life. When we
examine our fears closely, we see that they are mainly
based upon not being in control. I am afraid of heights.
On a recent trip to Egypt I took a balloon ride over the
Valley of the Kings. I was amazed that I felt no fear of
the heights as our balloon ascended over the valley. I
believe that it was because I was standing next to the
Egyptian balloon pilot, a veteran Egyptian Air Force
Officer. I felt that he had control of the balloon. In turn
I felt in control and was not bothered at all, or at any
time during the flight.

While not overlooking real and beneficial fears of

the everyday dangers of life, controlling unrealistic fears is a necessary psychic activity.

Most of us fear the wrong things and our fears generally are outsized in proportion to their real probability.

A year or so ago I talked with my son Brian about taking a trip with me to the Holy Land. My plan was to visit the historic sites in Israel and Jordan. Like most American's Brian thought I was crazy for wanting to visit what many view as such a dangerous place so he declined my offer.

I went anyway.

One day while in Jordan I stopped into a café in Petra. After exchanging the usual pleasantries that I have come to understand is the way of their culture the Arab shopkeeper asked me if I had any children. I told him that I had two. He told me he had 18. He asked me where they lived. I told him that my son lived in Chicago and before I could utter another word he grabbed his heart and said:

> *"How could you let your son live in the most dangerous place in the world? We see it on CNN. They kill people on streets for no reason".*

Fear is usually about perception. I know there are

places in Chicago that are as dangerous as that Arab shopkeeper was talking about, but I naturally and instinctively avoid them as does my son.

We just often don't understand that much of the world is the same way. There are places in some countries to avoid and there are times in safe countries that it is a good idea to stay inside.

It is all about perspective and while the televised images that are beamed around the world do not lie, they very often distort reality.

Learning when to be careful rather then fearful is a very hard thing to learn.

Worries

> *Worry distorts our thinking, disrupts our work, disquiets our soul, disturbs our body, disfigures our face, destroys our poise, depresses our friends, demoralizes our life, defeats our faith and debilitates our energy.*
>
> William A. Ward

Worrying is different from being prepared. Worrying is often anticipatory angst, the preliminary buying of trouble, an imagination on overdrive. Worrying is seeing trouble around every corner, potholes that may be out there in the dark, and crawly things under the bed.

Do not go there. Be prepared, anticipate dangers, but do not engage in causeless worrying. It will just take years from your life and joy from your day.

Anxiety

> *A pessimist is one who feels bad when he feels good for fear he will feel worse when he feels better.*
>
> *Unknown author*

Anxiety is so often unwarranted, but suppressing unnecessary angst is difficult until you learn to differentiate between big deals and little deals, and between things you can do something about, and things you have no control about.

Too often we engage in anticipatory angst about things, which while they have little odds of actually happening, we fear them so greatly that we are almost ready to surrender before a shot is fired.

Anxiety can suck the joy out of your day and happiness from your life and is to be avoided and not self-inflicted.

Most of the time the figurative gun at your head is often in your own hand.

On Envy

It is a wise (person) that does not grieve for the things, which he has not, but rejoice for those, which he has.

Epictetus

Envy is a source of unhappiness and unnecessary anguish. You should never let envy about what someone else has, rob you of the joy and happiness that you experience, from what you have.

Once you start to allow envy to effect you there are no limits to its insidious reach.

Be ever thankful for what you have without an envious thought of others. Envy and its accompanying jealously should have no place in your emotions or your heart.

This is one of the key wellsprings for finding happiness and joy in your life.

Mental Health

The mind is a bit like a garden. If it isn't fed and cultivated, weeds will take it over.

Erwin G. Hall

On Puzzles

The world is a fascinating puzzle full of memorable sights, sounds and smells. I have always been fascinated by both the differences and similarities to my native cultures. The people, language, cuisine, culture, customs, beliefs and folkways are endlessly fascinating, both timeless, and ever changing in equal measure.

I have tried to understand as much of it as I can and will continue to travel to every corner of our small planet. In my travels, I have tried to make no judgments on other cultures and though my stomach may sometimes revolt against strange foods, I will never tire of always seeking to absorb and understand this world through the eyes of the local inhabitants, rather than through my own inherent cultural bias and prejudicial beliefs.

You should never tire of being curious about life and the world in which we live. When you do tire and lose your curiosity you will have stopped living and are ready to roll over and die.

On Wisdom

That which the fool does in the end the wise person does in the beginning.

R. C. Trench

Wisdom doesn't come automatically with old age. Nothing does----except wrinkles. It's true, some wines improve with age. But only if the grapes were good in the first place.

Abigail Van Buren

Wisdom is knowing instinctively how to handle missing information, new situations, and seeing solutions were others only see problems.

Wisdom is not something that can necessarily be taught and you do not actually achieve it because you get older and possibly more mature, though it can contribute to it.

Wisdom is not to be obtained from textbooks, but must be coined out of human experience in the flame of life.

Morris Raphael Cohen

When someone has wisdom you can usually tell it, and conversely when wisdom is absent in someone it is also painfully obvious.

Wisdom is a collection of individual qualities, an understanding that every person we meet may know something useful that we don't know, and the inherent ability to figure out what is both true, and what truly matters.

Maturity

Maturity is not just about "been there---done that". It is more about "learned from" and "now understand".

Some people never get there. We can all fall subject to arrested development, of time-warpness, meaning we can reach a certain age and just stop growing and developing. Our hairstyle and wardrobe freezes in time and we spend the rest of our life locked in the fashions and attitudes at our stop point.

We all know people like this but we often do not necessarily recognize it when it is us who are frozen in time. We all can, and most likely probably will, all become out-of-touch in some aspect of our lives whether it is music, clothing, furniture, activities, attitudes or prejudices.

However, maturity has more to do with having mentally and attitudinally grown rather than concerning "tastes". We can live in a 200-year-old house and have habits of a bygone era, but if we are culturally aware and have an appreciation of lessons-learned from a well-spent life then we are mature.

Additionally, maturity can result in wisdom, but not necessarily, but at a minimum maturity needs to result in becoming an adult.

On Confidence

*Do not let what you cannot do interfere with
what you can do.*

John Wooden

Confidence is necessary to get up in the morning to
face the world. It is necessary to have the courage to try
anything new, whether it be something big like starting
a business or as mundane as trying a new food.

Confidence comes from within. It is a state of mind,
an attitude, as well as the face you give to the world.
It is what gets you through the day, sees you through
times of trouble, and lets you persevere in the face of
adversity, whether small or large.

There is a bad segues to confidence and that is
arrogance. Confidence is a realistic and grounded belief
in you, and your abilities and prospects. Arrogance is
a puffed-chest, ego-driven unrealistic and unfounded
form of confidence.

*There are two types of mental factors, which are
quite similar: one is self-confidence and the other
is conceit or pride. Both of them are similar in
that they are uplifting states of mind, which give
you a certain degree of confidence and boldness.
But conceit and pride tend to more negative
consequences, whereas self-confidence tends to*

lead to more positive consequences.

14th Dali Lama

Always keep your confidence restrained and be ever watchful to not let it cross the line into arrogance.

On Thinking

The energy of the mind is the essence of life.

Aristotle

An open mind is the beginning of self-discovery and growth. We can't learn anything new until we can admit that we don't already know everything.

Erwin G. Hall

The things you think about determine the quality of your life. Your soul takes on the color of your thoughts.

Marcus Aurelius

Nurture your mind with great thoughts, for you will never go any higher than you think.

Benjamin Disraeli

Your mind is your greatest asset and it is the only one that you have that can be deployed to achieve happiness and joy in your life. It can help you focus on what is truly important, help you in changing your attitudes, help you to be tolerant and understanding in your dealings with other people.

Never be afraid to say "I will need to think about it" when faced with a decision.

And never, ever, think that you know it all; no matter how wise you think you may have become.

While you will develop strong opinions and beliefs over time you will cheat yourself if you are not willing to listen to new ideas and thoughts, even if they contradict long held beliefs. If your reasoning behind your viewpoint is strong enough it will only become stronger if you are willing to listen to alternatives and countervailing arguments.

Your mind and heart should always be open to listening to others.

On Possibilities

The saying that life is full of endless possibilities is something that American's believe in and is almost a national motto. Of course, the circumstances of our birth tend to reduce many of those possibilities almost immediately, so it is a "qualified" motto at best.

In order for possibilities to be realized there must be opportunities, but as the noted Chinese philosopher said:

Opportunities multiply as they are seized.

Sun Tzu

While you may see the opportunities, you may also often lack the operative vision, resources and courage to seize on the opportunity and to make it happen. This is a normal reality and we all will be in circumstances that prevent us from taking advantage of opportunities when they are presented.

When I was a young father I had the dream, drive and the opportunity to finish my education and get a PhD. It was a dream I had nurtured since my freshman year in college. It was not to be. Instead the responsibility of providing for my daughter, a stay-at-home, non-working pregnant wife and a soon-to-be-born son required me to postpone my dream and to get a full time job.

While that decision closed one career door it eventually led to the opening of new ones that I had never imagined. Later I would spend 11 years being a part-time instructor of Political Science at a local Junior College, but my dream of being a professor became an ever-fading dream.

I am not sure when it eventually died, but it did, and that's OK.

Dreams

So what are dreams? We all have them, and I am not talking about the dreams we have when we sleep; I'm talking about the ones we have when we sit alone staring into space.

> *Nothing happens unless it is first a dream.*
>
> *Carl Sandburg*

> *Dream no small dreams for they have no power to move the hearts of men.*
>
> *Goethe*

> *Follow your dreams and pursue them with courage for it is the pursuit of those dreams that makes life really worth living.*
>
> *Lind DuPuy Moore*

Dreams are part hope, part yearning, and part desire. It is what we wish for if we could just wave the wand.

Dreams are usually unformed and not necessarily what we are actively seeking. Often we do not mention our dreams because they seem so impossible, so unachievable, that we fear ridicule from our family and friends should we utter them.

We usually have not elevated our dreams into possibilities that we can actively imagine happening. They often lie quiet, in the back of our minds, or hidden away in a drawer like some great secret.

Imagination

Imagination is more important than knowledge.

Albert Einstein

Imagination will often carry us to worlds that never were, but without it we go nowhere.

Carl Sagan

We are what we imagine ourselves to be.

Kurt Vonnegut

Do what you love and the money will follow

Marsha Sinetar

When we move beyond just dreaming and begin actively trying to achieve our dreams, we begin to channel our dreams into imagining something new, maybe even something unique.

Imagining is where we create something new, which is partly from our dreams, partly from an opportunity we see, or feel is there, and partly from a special creative space that lies in all of us. For many of us this imagination will never come forward into the light of day. For others is bubbles to the surface occasionally and in spurts, often to die an unrealized thought in the light of a new day and the crush of day-to-day living.

For still others though, imagination and the flow of creative juices is a very common and everyday presence. It surges through ones veins and is as regular as the tides in the ocean or a thunderstorm that spawns little tornado sub-thoughts and imaginings.

Discovery

Discovery consists of seeing what everybody has seen and thinking what nobody has thought.

Albert Szent-Gyorgyi

Some of the world's greatest feats were accomplished by people not smart enough to know they were impossible.

Doug Larson

Discovery is what lies under that rock that your fertile imagination tells you to turn over. It is the unknown that lies behind the door, around the corner, and over the next hill.

It can neither be sought nor imagined. It must be found.

It then traverses full circle and opens up new possibilities.

And so on...

> *Don't keep forever on the public road, going only where others have gone. Leave the beaten track occasionally and dive into the woods. You will be certain to find something you have never seen before. It will be a little thing, but do not ignore it. Follow it up, explore all around it; one discovery will lead to another, and before you know it you will have something worth thinking about.*
>
> *Alexander Graham Bell*

On Rationality

Whenever we initially label a situation or a person in a certain way we often then become unable to see them differently. In effect we put on a set of irrational blinders that filter out any contradictory information that subsequently comes our way that conflicts with our original assessments.

You should never lose sight of the fact that no matter how intelligent we think we are that our core beliefs and attitudes are not the result of rational or conscious decisions that we just somehow came up with on our own.

We are social creatures and are heavily influenced by the geography and circumstances of our birth and upbringing. The country, class, culture, family and economic circumstances determine in large measure what we believe in and how we view the world. We can change some of our beliefs and attitudes by conscious thoughts and changes in circumstances but for most people this does not happen.

Thus we judge others though an irrational prism and we should never lose sight of this fact, and the fact that they look back at us through a reverse prism of their own.

I have often wondered what the people in other countries are thinking about me and my traveling companions as we journey through their lands in our sleek little buses staring at them and snapping pictures at their strange dress and culture. I can't help but think how odd and exotic we must seem to them.

Social Health

Learning to well live with others is what separates humans from animals. We are by nature social creatures that must learn behaviors to practice and avoid to remain human.

On Pleasantness

If noise bothers you then you need to create a quiet oasis for your sanity. Or if crowds steal your joy avoid them. Whatever the surrounding environmental conditions that you do not like---do not feel compelled to put up with it.

I believe it is OK to avoid that which you do not like, and savor that which you do, and you should not let anyone tell you otherwise. That which makes you unhappy is bad. That which makes you happy is good. As long as you are doing no harm by doing what you like as opposed to what others want, or expect you to do, then it is your call.

I enjoy being completely alone in the early pre-dawn hours with no noise except the birds waking. Some people have told me that this is anti-social. I do not buy that. It is an individual preference. Nothing more. Of course, it can be carried to an extreme, like anything else, and is a sign of anti-social behavior. But in a mad and violent world, I think it is a rather harmless version of antisocial behavior.

Secure whatever form of peaceful environment that makes you happy and do not listen to anyone else.

We all have situations that it is best for us to avoid.

The conscious avoidance of unpleasantness is a requisite thing to do to maintain your happiness bubble. We all too often feel that we have to do certain things, be around situations that we would rather avoid.

You must understand that not only can you walk away from unpleasantness, but that you should. Whether it is a fight, a confrontation or just a simple argument----just walk away.

We all have toxic people who enter our lives. A toxic person is anyone that you do not like to be around, or you should not, be around. They take away from your happiness, your joy, and your life.

By toxicity, I do not mean the mild irritations that all of us experience from other people. Even the most loving of relationships experience many moments of friction. It goes with the human psyche.

One type of toxic person can anger you, make you want to scream, and drives up your blood pressure at their very sight or the sound of their voice. They literally suck the air out of your happiness bubble.

A second kind of toxic person is milder but just as deadly to your soul. The person encourages you in the wrong kind of behavior, befriends you with the wrong kind of advice, and takes you in mentally and physically wrong directions. They are catalysts for bad decisions but since you acquiesce in the actions, you are the author of your own bad decisions.

The third kind of toxic person is the attention demander, the perpetual whiner, and the one that is serially unhappy, wants you to take note of their misery, and demands your attention. They can wear you down and rob you of your own joy for life.

Some are relatives that you cannot totally avoid, but you can devise ways to lessen either your time with them or their ability to negatively affect you.

Others are coworkers, friends, or neighbors. The degree to which you can avoid or eliminate contact, and therefore toxic effect, is dependent up how much contact you "must" have, and how creative you can be in avoidance.

On Friends

A true friendship develops on the basis of genuine human affection, not money or power. Of course, due to your power or wealth, more people may approach you with big smiles or gifts. But deep down these are not real friends of yours; these are friends of your wealth or power. As long as your fortune remains, then these people will often approach you. But when your fortune decline, they will no longer be there.

14th Dali Lama

A friend is a person with whom I may be sincere.

Ralph Waldo Emerson

A real friend is one who walks in when the rest of the world walks out.

Walter Winchell

Genuine friendships are something that we all seek. Knowing the true from the false is something we just learn, as we get older, and hopefully wiser.

Since we can inadvertently pick up the habits, outlooks and beliefs from the people we associate with we should be careful about the company we keep. We are all well aware of how friends can lead us astray and as we grow older we learn this lesson either from personal experience or by observation.

It is vitally important to keep in mind that just because people are nice to you doesn't mean you have to spend time with them. The same holds true for coworkers and other people with whom we associate.

We should be selective about whom we take as friends. They can affect your future and your happiness. Choose only those who uplift you and bring out the best in you. Do not let someone else's sorrow or bad course affect your life. Though many people mean well it doesn't mean they should be in your life.

Friends are a choice thing and among the biggest decisions in your lives. Bad choices can steal the thunder from your life.

On Enemies

A wise man gets more use from his enemies than a fool from his friends.

Baltasar Gracian

Enemies give us the opportunity to practice patience and with the opportunity to display tolerance. We should look upon those who try to harm us, or on those who should be avoided else they do us harm, as good teachers.

Enemies and danger keep you alert, keep you from becoming complacent, and if they try to do you harm out of misguided ignorance or misunderstanding they are more to be pitied then scorned.

When your alertness prepares you to take counter-measures against the danger you can do so without anger. Thus, the actions, which are taken out of wisdom rather than anger and hatred, are usually more effective.

When you defeat an enemy you should treat them with magnanimity rather then trying to heap humiliation upon them for to do otherwise is to keep lit the fire in their hearts for retribution or revenge.

And always keep in mind that a person can be judged more by who their enemies are, than by whom their friends are. If you accumulate enemies in life by standing up for what is right and always seeking to do good then your enemies will probably be evil people.

You will thus be relatively certain that you have lived a good life.

On Family

We are all rooted in family---it is the soil from which we sprang and the ground upon which we stand.

Susan Piver

Your family can be a great source of comfort and fulfillment or an equally great contributor to angst, unhappiness and sorrow. It is one of the most fundamental parts of our life. No matter what we do in life, we cannot undo the family past into which we are born. We inherent psychological, social, and attitudinal inclinations from our family, along with our genetic characteristics. We may later strike out as individuals, who are unique and different from the inherited inclinations that we receive from our families, but for those who don't seek to be different, family forms a bond, community, and heritage that is often very comfortable just to accept as is without question.

When traveling in rural Jordan I was struck by the sameness in dress, houses, food and activities of many of the people as my tour bus would make occasional stops through the countryside. Part of me was repelled by the appearance of the woman in their black robes that covered their heads and bodies in the traditional manner. I felt that for some it might be a prison environment. That surely they must feel locked into a way of life for which they had no control. While some may feel that way----do they all? Is it possible that many, if not most, are content and happy within the bonds, and protective certainty, of family, community and tradition.

I believe that it is not for me, or for you, to decide for others. While some people are trapped within a family life that they want to break away from it, individualism can only occur if it is driven and sought by the individual.

It is all about your attitude and the luck of your circumstances. Luck in that most of who is in your family occurs outside of your control. Nevertheless, you do control your attitude about the menagerie that is your family.

All families are probably similar to yours---the good, the bad and the ugly. Add to that the occasional crazy and troublesome relatives we all have to endure at various points in our lives.

To deal with your family you should develop an attitude of amusement, and appreciation, in equal measure.

Cherish the good and endure the other with humor as your best defense. It is better than crying or anger.

Never think that only you have people like some of those that you have in your family. The laws governing the random distribution of human nature create quite similar family members among your friends, neighbors, and coworkers.

In the end your immediate family are the ones you should always be able to look to for your closest support, assistance, and solace in a cold and increasingly impersonal world.

In the best of circumstances, your family is the core of your existence in this world and you should continually nurture your familial relationships.

On Honor

Honor wears different coats to different eyes.

Barbara Tuchman

Being a person of honor is the way to a more meaningful, satisfying life, regardless of society's failings. We gain self-respect by setting our own standards and holding ourselves accountable to them. We gain clarity and confidence by knowing which lines we will not cross. And we gain nobility by paying heed to principles larger then ourselves.

James P. Owen

The word honor can be one of the best words or one of the worst. Like religion honor can be a cause for good, or for evil. Honor is an explosive word. It can be a reason for good deeds or the justification for bad deeds.

Examples:

"Code of honor" sounds like a good thing---it depends what the code says you should do to maintain the honor.

"Badge of honor" can be a good thing that can become a reason for doing a bad thing.

"Honor killings" is unquestionably a bad thing.

Dignity

Dignity is the ability of a person to live with their head held up without shame or humiliation.

You should always conduct yourself with an appreciation of the dignity needs of others and always be willing to do what you can to afford every person you come in contact with their measure of dignity.

Learn the ways to be charitable without harm, magnanimous without boasting, and celebratory without arrogance.

And never lose your own dignity in a squabble with someone who is not worthy. Have pity on such people and not scorn.

On Arguments

... anger sinks into the soul and remains for a long time

Epictetus

A disagreement with coworkers, neighbors and loved ones is a life constant. There is no avoiding not agreeing sometimes, with someone.

Controlling anger requires awareness and a then a degree of learned behavior.

Anger

The ultimate source of my mental happiness is my peace of mind. Nothing can destroy this except my own anger.

14th Dali Lama

The greatest remedy for anger is delay.

Seneca

Never insult an alligator until after you have crossed the river.

Cordell Hull

Magnanimity

Anyone can become angry. That is easy. But to be angry with the right person, to the right degree, at the right time, for the right purpose and in the right way---that is not easy.

Aristotle

You do not possess your emotions. They possess you.

Winston Churchill

Nothing gives one person so much advantage over another as to remain always cool and unruffled under all circumstances.

Thomas Jefferson

A person who is secure remains in control of their emotions and knows how to temper their tempers.

Whenever you win at a game or in life always reach out to the one you have defeated, not with superiority, but with a sense of humility. Never brag nor display a sense that you are superior in your victory, but rather be humble and let your success speak for itself.

On Trust

When we come into this world as a fragile infant we have no choice than to trust in others to be nourished and kept alive. This will continue your entire life and you will be having that trust sometimes betrayed. It can no more be avoided than can bad weather. We learn to be appropriately wary and cautious with our trust but we should never have our heart become so hardened by disappointment that we think we can never trust another again.

Time heals most wounds and cautious optimism is usually the best route to happiness. The alternative brings with itself another kind of sour baggage.

Always be willing to cautiously give someone your trust again, even when they have disappointed you, but with the clear admonishment and understanding that you are taking a chance.

On Reputation

If you wish to be well spoken of, learn to speak well of others

Epictetus

We cannot control the evil tongues of others; but a good life enables us to disregard them

Cato

The greatest gift I received from my father was his reputation. I have honored him by living my life in such a way as to give my children the same heritage.

My father was an honest and honorable man. To him his word, his reputation, and his promises meant a everything. He always believed in doing the right thing, of treating all people with respect, and being proper in behavior at all times.

Our reputation can serve us well or it can serve us ill. It has the power to open doors as well as to close them. It is the foundation and the image of who we are.

Your reputation is built over time by your deeds and actions, but it is a fragile thing. It can be damaged, and in some cases destroyed, by a single particularly egregious mistake. While sometimes this can occur because of a false accusation or misunderstanding, it most often occurs because we slip up and do something really stupid.

Unfortunately we often don't see the damage coming, but we certainly notice it afterwards by the disappointing stares of friends and family.

The maintenance of a good reputation requires due diligence concerning your conduct and behavior. Once your reputation is damaged it becomes a struggle to rebuild it, but yes, it can be done.

You must forgive yourself in the process.

On Solitude

Solitude is important to man. It is necessary to his achievement of peace and contentment. It is a well into which he dips for refreshment of his soul.

Margaret E. Mulac

Being alone does not mean being lonely. It means cutting off the external, the superficial and the superfluous, and seeking instead the inner strength, which one finds best in solitude.

Henry King

Not all of us like being alone. I am one who not only enjoys it, but I relish it. Among my favorite sayings is:

The happiest of all lives is a busy solitude.

Voltaire

Solitude nourishes my soul. It lets me think and to reflect. It gives me the opportunity and space to put things into perspective, to plan and to prepare.

Silence

The word "listen" contains the same letter as the word "silent".

Alfred Brendel

The most important thing in communications is to hear what isn't being said.

Peter F. Drucker

Sometimes the news is in the noise, and sometimes the news is in the silence.

Thomas L. Friedman

I have always found silence to be preferable to meaningless chattiness. While I probably carry silence to the extreme there is much to be said, as an old saying goes:

It is better to remain silent and have people think that you are a fool, then to open your mouth and remove all doubt.

Author unknown

Memories

Life is not measured by the breaths we take or the riches we have, but by the memories that fill our hearts and are so extraordinary that they sometimes take our breath away.

Jane Middleton Moz

Our memories cannot be taken from us. They stay in our mind and our heart until age and infirmity begin to jumble and fade them. But while we have them they bring a smile to our face or a tear to our eyes when something triggers them.

You should think about what causes your negative memories and endeavor to avoid, and/or eliminate the triggers that bring about sadness. Alternately, you can mentally re-program the negative triggers towards more positive memories. If a certain holiday brings a bad memory to your unconsciousness, try to begin consciously associating it with a new, replacement memory.

Memories are like disk space ---- they can be overwritten.

Reflections

Occasionally we need to take a pause to reflect on where we are, measure our status, and decide on our next steps. This is something we should learn to do naturally whenever we reach a fork in the road of life, or see an approaching dead end.

Reflection requires us to hear the small voice in our head that is speaking out to us and says, "Stop a minute, and think about this". There is a Zen expression that says:

> *You cannot see your reflection in moving water,*
> *only in still water.*

> *Unknown author*

Find a quiet place to tune out the distractions that are clouding your thoughts. The goal is to clarify your thoughts.

Taking the time regularly to reflect upon and adjust your attitudes, as well as your directions, is an essential ingredient to both reaching your intended destinations and for your general long- term happiness.

Values Health

Values are beliefs and attitudes about what is good, right, desirable and worthwhile in the world. They are internal convictions that support our movement through life. Our value systems are like maps in our hearts that give us direction for our judgments and choices

Jane Middleton-Moz

A healthy attitude is essential to happiness. Much can be overcome with a proper attitude about the flow of life.

On Humility

Never seem more learned than the people you are with. Wear your learning like a pocket watch and keep it hidden. Do not pull it out to count the hours, but give the time when you are asked.

Lord Chesterfield

None are so empty as those who are full of themselves.

Benjamin Whichcote

When someone sings his own praises, he always gets the tune too high.

Mary H. Waldrip

It is unhealthy to marinate in your own press clippings.

Sam Walton

Noise proves nothing. Often a hen who has merely laid an egg cackles as if she had laid an asteroid.

Mark Twain

Humble people don't profess that they know everything; they don't brag about themselves and their exploits; they don't think they are always right; and they don't pass judgment on other people.

Non-humble people do just the opposite, and they do so primarily out of their lack of self-confidence. Best rule of thumb is that whatever someone forcefully brags about is usually not completely true.

Pride

Pride is one of those attitudes that by itself is not necessarily bad. It is the manifestations of pride that cause us trouble. Pride can be a simple glow or good feeling in an accomplishment, or characteristic that we have like ethnicity or a team that we belong to.

Pride becomes negative when we become arrogant about it, or express it in a superior way, usually to the derision of others.

Pride is best when displayed in a mellow versus a harsh way. And you should always let others have the opportunity for their own display and actualizations of their unique pride.

Self-Centeredness

When science discovers the center of the universe, a lot of people will be disappointed to find they are not it.

Bernard Baily

Pre-occupation with self is endemic in the 21st

century Western World, but especially in America. The media bombard us daily with reasons to glorify our bodies, our homes, and everything about ourselves. Business leaders, athletes and entertainers, fed by their PR machines, crank out reams of self-glorification stories with pictures and multi-media presentations.

Narcissism is the term for this type of behavior. Avoid it by replacing "I" with "we" whenever possible in your writing and in your speech. Be aware and vigilant of your behavior and correct yourself when you notice any trends toward attitudes that are too much about "me" rather then about "we".

On Patience

Patience is the ability to idle your motor when you feel like stripping your gears.

Michael LeFan

Patience is the ability to relax and recognize the things in life, which are not within our control, those things which we cannot change. When you have patience you have realistically adjusted your expectations of others, yourself, situations and the general flow of life.

Patience is a mind-set, a way of coping with the daily grind of life. It is realizing how unimportant, both in the long-term, but often in the short-term, are the constant irritating delays that occur regularly in our life. The more we can cultivate patience, the happier and more relaxed we become.

The main way I keep patient is first to keep my sense of humor.

In transiting the airport in Delhi, India I was in the exiting immigration line for over an hour because I happened to get in the line with the laziest passport officer I have ever encountered. He was an older government official, the kind that in the Indian system cannot be fired no matter what they do so long as they show up to work. I thought to myself that the slow official at the passport line that is keeping me waiting for an hour when I could be just waiting at my plane's gate. No point in being impatient. I had several hours till my flight left and this was my last hurdle till I got to my gate. I just watched how slow he was, was amused as he stopped to chat with the passengers ahead and smiled at how funny the irritated people in line were---like getting through this line quickly is going to gain them something.

Patience will serve you well and is itself an antidote to frenzied busyness with little gain.

On Empathy

Empathy is the ability to sincerely understand how other people feel. To be truly empathic you must be aware of, and sensitive to others feelings, whether you agree with the source, or the cause of those feelings. What is important is not your feelings, but theirs.

Compassion

> *How far you go in life depends on your being tender with the young, compassionate with the aged, sympathetic with the striving, and tolerant of the weak and the strong -- because someday you will have been all of these.*
>
> *George Washington Carver*

Compassion it what makes us truly human. All religions teach compassion to our fellow human beings, and though often-religious practice may fall short of the ideal, few will argue against the notion that compassion is, and should be, about all human business. Compassion is not pity. Pity is disdain or the feeling that people need to be fixed or repaired. Compassion requires that we genuinely feel the pain of others and want to sincerely assist them in relieving the pain or suffering.

Compassion is shared suffering.

Charity

Give what you have. To some one it may be better than you dare to think.

Henry Waldsworth Longfellow

What do we live for if not to make the world less difficult for each other?

George Eliot.

Charity is not merely the giving of money and our time to some worthy or needy cause; it is the giving of our hearts to make the lives of others better. If you give money to charity and it is not a sacrifice then you have not given enough. Give till it begins to hurt. Only then will the gift be sincere.

Kindness

Make a rule....never to lie down at night without being able to say; "I have made one human being at least a little wiser, or a little happier, or at least a little better this day."

Charles Kingsley

Kindness to others is one of the easiest things that one human being can give to another. Being gentle and helpful to other people will nourish your soul and does not cost you a thing.

Being kind to others, especially to strangers, is a prime indicator of a person's character.

Listening

If we were supposed to talk more than we listen, we would have two mouths and one ear.

Mark Twain

Good listening is the key to empathy. It acknowledges that the other person has something worth saying. By listening you are giving worth to their thoughts and to their feelings. You are saying that they matter.

Hearing is not the same as listening. Listening is hard for most of us because it requires us to focus on the needs and feelings of the other person.

Listen quietly and allow the other persons thoughts or feelings to sink in. Let them percolate for a bit before you make any comments. Do not begin forming counter-opinions while they are talking. Do not interrupt them. Do not let your prejudices and biases on ideas get in the way of listening. You should always be open to countervailing thoughts, no matter how initially ridiculous they may seem at first. How else will you ever learn anything?

Good listening comes from the heart.

On Forgiving

There is no passion of the human heart that promises so much and pays so little as that of revenge.

H. B. Shaw

Doing an injury puts you below your enemy; revenging one makes you but even with him; forgiving it sets you above him.

Benjamin Franklin

Forgiveness is one of the most difficult values to have, but it can be one of the most important for your individual happiness. Resentments, hurts, and ill feelings become an ever-heavier load to carry and they can suck the joy out of living.

Forgiveness is not about condoning hurtful or harmful behavior by others. You don't have to pretend that everything is just fine. It is not a sign of reconciliation or weakness on your part.

Forgiveness is a process of letting go of the past, of healing and moving on with our lives.

Resentment is poison to your soul.

Pain is inevitable. Misery is optional.

Tim Hansel

You will have many opportunities in your life to be forgiving and each one will afford you different levels of pain and challenge.

It is always the better person that finds forgiveness in their heart, and it will nourish your soul.

The most difficult person to forgive is often yourself.

To achieve happiness in life you must forgive yourself for your indiscretions, bad decisions, and all foot-in-mouth behaviors.

On Courage

Courage is being scared to death----and saddling up anyway.

John Wayne

Life shrinks or expands in proportion to one's courage

Anais Nin

Very ordinary things paralyze many of us and we go through life surviving but never really living as our heart wills us to do so. We are often ruled by fear, doubt, and worry.

No one is born with courage. It is something that must be acquired through experiences over time.

Courage is often necessary in order to care for others even when it involves risk to yourselves. Additionally, it takes courage to speak the truth, to stand up for one's principles, to protect the weak, and to fight injustice.

One form of courage that never goes out of style is moral courage, yet often it seems so lacking in contemporary society. Moral courage is standing up for what is right, in doing what is right. It means not ignoring injustice, nor walking away from a virtuous fight.

On Humor

A person without a sense of humor is like a wagon without springs. Every pebble on the road jolts it.

Henry Ward Beecher

Laughter is the sun that drives winter from the human face.

Victor Hugo

Laughter gives us distance. It allows us to step back from an event, deal with it and then move on.

Bob Newhart

Life can be stressful enough without taking every event, every encounter, and everything that comes your way too seriously. Keeping your sense of humor and appreciation for the absurd is an essential ingredient to avoiding unnecessary and unproductive stress.

You should approach life with a smile and an acceptance of whatever happens with good humor and ironic appreciation.

On Tolerance

Tolerance is acceptance of the view, beliefs and cultural identity of others. It is the acceptance and appreciation of the differences in others: traditions, cultures, languages, spiritual beliefs and so on. It does not imply agreement with others' points of view, but rather respect for others' rights to their beliefs.

Jane Middleton Moz

One of the main sources of conflict in the world is intolerance. It manifests itself in hatred and derision of others who have a different race, religion, ethnic ways, beliefs, or lifestyles.

These conflicts based upon intolerance are as old as the history of the human race and are unlikely to change in the near future.

Tolerance is an acceptance that the world both at large, and immediately around you is full of different people, with different beliefs, attitudes and values. Further, that these people have a right to their way of life so long as it does not interfere with my rights, to live my life, my way.

If you travel the world tolerance becomes a necessary precursor to understanding the varying cultures of the world, many of whom are themselves intolerant of other peoples, beliefs and cultures.

You should always keep in mind that others whom you encounter in your travels have a very different worldview and natural cultural bias then you do. Further that thier view have been shaped by a set of firmly held beliefs and that they will look upon you with the same sense of bewilderment that you do upon them.

There is no all encompassing right and wrong cultural, religious or behavioral way to live except for the basic tenents of doing no harm to others and treating all people with respect and dignity.

On Truth

We can easily forgive a child who is afraid of the dark; the real tragedy of life is when men are afraid of the light.

Plato

Fear is a natural reaction to moving closer to the truth.

Pema Chodron

Being truthful requires us to often choose the most difficult of choices.

We all profess that truthfulness is a value to be followed even when we know we don't and in modern American society there are far too many examples of blatant untruthfulness in all walks of life.

Honesty

Honesty has a beautiful and refreshing simplicity about it. No ulterior motives. No hidden meanings. An absence of hypocrisy, duplicity, political games, and verbal superficiality.

Chuck Swindoll

Honesty is essential to achieving virtue, self-respect and honor, and is among the hardest of character traits to achieve. As a young man I learned that most everyone that knew my father respected him most of all for his honesty. What is most remarkable is that he spent most of his life selling things to people, from his days of running the town grocery store in our home town of Oakford, Illinois to his days selling fence products in Florida until he retired. In between he sold cigars, cars and whatever else he could peddle. He was the most honest person I have ever known in my life and I honor his example.

Honesty has a dark side though. We often can't handle the truth and my father was not immune from the need to tell the "white lie", or what I prefer to refer to as truth suppression or avoidance----just not telling people things that will just upset them. It is sometimes necessary to not have people be fully informed.

Integrity

> *Integrity means you do what is right and not just fashionable or politically correct. A life of principle, of not succumbing to the seductive sirens of an easy morality, will always win the day.*
>
> *Denis Waitley*

> *There can be no happiness if the things we believe in are different from the things we do.*
>
> *Freya Stark*

The time is always right to do what is right.

Martin Luther King, Jr.

I have always conducted my professional life with an internal sense of integrity, not just because it was the right thing, but because I wanted to never provide an embarrassment either to my family or those who trusted me.

On Appreciation

We never appreciate the value of water until the well runs dry.

Benjamin Franklin

You should always demonstrate by word and deed your true appreciation for all that you receive from others. You should never take the attitude that anything is ever expected, nor that you deserve anything from anyone.

As we express our gratitude, we must never forget that the highest appreciation is not to utter words but to live by them.

John F. Kennedy

Further, you should treat all people from whom you receive a service or kindness from with equal appreciation, from the highest to the lowest stations in life. Neither the giver nor the receiver should ever be viewed as the better. Appreciation should be based on equality between the giver and the receiver.

Gratitude

I wept because I had no shoes, until I saw a man who had no feet.

Think of life as if it were a banquet where you would behave graciously. When dishes are passed to you, extend your hand and help yourself to a moderate portion. If a dish should pass you by, enjoy what is already on your plate. Or if the dish hasn't been passed to you yet, patiently wait your turn.

Epictetus

Gratitude is appreciation and patience. It is about waiting your turn, taking a share of whatever is offered and appreciating what you have. Practicing polite restraint and appreciation in all of your endeavors is a characteristic that will separate you from others and help contribute to a life of satisfied moderation in all things.

The older you get and the more you see of the world, the more you appreciate what you have and how lucky you are to live a safe and secure existence in boring middle class middle-America.

Gratitude unlocks the fullness of life. It turns what we have into enough, and more. It turns denial into acceptance, chaos to order, and confusion to clarity. It can turn a meal into a feast, a house into a home, a stranger into a friend. Gratitude makes sense of our past, brings peace for today, and creates a vision for tomorrow.

Melody Beattie

Physical Health

He who has health has hope, and he who has hope has everything.

Arabian Proverb

On Vitality

Vitality is the essential life force that nourishes us and gives us our drive. As we age, our reservoir of vital energy becomes depleted by the wear and tear, and difficulties, of our daily lives.

Living well is critically dependent upon your vitality level. It is affected primarily by three essential factors----your living/working environment, other people, and you.

You can control the effect of all three. You cannot do it completely, but you can do it enough, and you will be better off trying than wallowing in self-pity and blame. What is essential is that you have a positive attitude toward your ability to control those elements that affect your vitality. The worst thing you can do is to whine about your woes and feel powerless.

Without vitality we cannot have the energy and self-discipline necessary to take control of our lives, to live consciously and to control our impulsive behaviors.

Negative thoughts and statements can reduce your self-esteem and sap your vitality. They can also lead us into bad choices in our physical and mental lives.

We are very fragile creatures and as we age, we

become ever more fragile. Bad behavior on our part can diminish our bodies and our spirit. We know the major things that we should not do, and we need not repeat that here in depth. All thinking adults know about substance abuse, smoking, being fat, not getting adequate exercise, and eating foods that are known to cause problems.

Physical health is extremely important to maintaining vitality as we age. I find myself noting frail elderly people at stores and shops as they try to navigate and move about with as much independence and dignity as possible.

The quality of any extra years is vitally important and I decided that it is not too late to begin a physical regime that anticipates those years. We will all get more fragile and frail as we age. Some simple changes in exercise, weight control and diet can decrease that frailty substantially. I believe that a disciplined lifestyle is more important in our retirement years than at any other time period of our life. Your margin for error is gone when you are old.

On Diet

Make your manner of eating neither luxurious nor gloomy, but lively and frugal...

Epictetus

Most intelligent and knowledgeable adults in the western world know how they should eat in order to maintain their health and avoid diet-related problems. That does not stop us from making diet books among the most popular items at the bookstore. We are a food-obsessed people in so many respects.

I believe in moderation in all things, that nothing is necessarily taboo. Delicious and bountiful food is to be enjoyed with a clear understanding of the consequences of overindulgence in things that are bad for you or non-consumption of healthful nutrients your body needs.

The rules on maintaining a proper weight are very simple----when you start to get fat then eat less and move more.

But do not deprive yourself completely. It will only make the food binges greater.

On Aging

A long life may not be good enough but a good life is long enough.

Benjamin Franklin

When we are young, we lie about our age by adding years to our real age because we want to seem older. When we are older, we begin to obfuscate our real age and periodically deny its steady advance over the years. Along the path into our older years, we experience the occasional angst over the milestone birthdays that signal our declining options and perceived capabilities.

American society does not necessarily honor the aged with acknowledgement of greater wisdom and inherent respect. Since we depict getting, "old" as a problem to be dealt with most of us avoid being categorized as being or approaching the category.

When we finally begin crossing the 60 barrier, we begin to become potentially more in denial about our real age. Middle-age comb-over's and body masking clothing give way to hyper-activity to prove that we remain vigorous and seemingly youthful.

I am 60 and I feel it. I decided a long time ago to be and act my age. While I take very good care of myself in order to keep energetic and to avoid long-term frailty, I refuse to color my gray or to engage in age-inappropriate behavior or to ever be in denial of my real age.

My knees hurt from the arthritis that we will all one day have. My eyesight is not as good as it once was but my hearing is holding up. I eat better and exercise appropriately and I try not to overdo anything.

One of the great dilemmas of living is that you do not know how long you are going to live. I am counting on having 10-15 "good" years followed by another 10+ years of declining years. Beyond that, I am not going to plan nor worry about it. It will be what it is going to be.

My basic advice on aging is just to enjoy whatever age you are at and just act your age at all times.

Life is long if it is full.

Seneca

On Exercise

Fitness is a key to an enjoyable life, but it goes without saying that most of us exercise less then we should, especially the older we get.

As we age this tendency to get out of shape gets more difficult to reverse unless we take conscious efforts to exercise our bodies regularity, and sometimes vigorously.

I find that I can get enough exercise by just putting physical exertion back into my daily life. I take the stairs and avoid elevators, I park as far from the entrance to a store as I can, I take every opportunity I can to lift heavy objects, and I take walks throughout my day just to exercise. If I can keep this up, I will not need to go to a health club. Instead, I can spend the money on good walking shoes and a rain jacket.

I have weights and small exercise devices scattered around my house and have conditioned myself to doing things like: curling barbells while waiting for my coffee to brew, doing a few repetitions on a rowing machine while waiting for a cooking timer to go off.

On Resting

Never be afraid to sit awhile and think.

Lorraine Hansberry

A holiday gives one a chance to look backward and forward, to reset oneself by an inner compass.

May Sarton

Resting allows us to refocus our priorities and ourselves. It is not a luxury. It is a necessity

Being tired can become chronic and problematic. Not only do you not function as well as you can when you are tired, but you leave yourself open to making sometimes very serious mistakes. Hard work does not have to result in rehabilitating tiredness. We often become less productive, not more productive, when you work long hours without rest. There is a misguided machismo about burning the midnight oil that pervades some work arenas.

Take your assigned tasks one by one, focus on each one intently, and then rest awhile before moving onto the next assigned task.

Spiritual Health

Spiritual health does not necessarily refer to any kind of religious faith. Spiritual health means the basic human good qualities of human affection, sense of involvement, honesty, and discipline guided by good motivation.

Religion I take to be concerned with faith claims to salvation of one faith or tradition or another.

Spirituality I take to be concerned with those qualities of the human spirit.

Dalai Lama

On Meaning

The quest for meaning and purpose in life is one of the most enduring endeavors that humans ever take. Wherever one travels in the world one will see ample evidence of this quest in ancient and modern monuments, behaviors and writings. It is something that is both intricately woven into spiritual beliefs yet often separate from the divine.

In the secular society of today this quest manifests itself in many forms. Traditions are receding ever more in importance----most of us have few anchors to hold us in place. This freedom can be a scary and lonely place. Because of this lack of traditional anchors we can fall victim to fads and cults that have "the answer", the magic meaning bullet, the simple answer to this ageless quest we all have to find meaning in our lives, in our existence.

You don't need to over think this. Meaning and purpose in life can be found in very simple, yet very profound ways. A loving companion, good friends, meaningful and rewarding work, and simple happiness can be sufficient meaning. We do not require anything more profound to give meaning to our lives.

Do not think that you must understand the deeper mysteries of life and its purposes to be happy.

Most of us are not sage philosophers that require great intellectual understanding of "the meaning of life". Most of us will not achieve greatness or notoriety in our lives. We will not achieve fame or fortune. Comfort and happiness will suffice to give our life meaning. If we experience love, companionship, fulfillment and enjoy ourselves during our passage on earth that may be good enough to have said that you have led a meaningful life.

On Beliefs

A belief is not merely an idea the mind possesses;
it is an idea that possesses the mind.

Robert Bolton

The world is a full of contrary beliefs, visions, viewpoints, and recriminations with no end to the shouting about the true way, the only way, or the only truth.

Most beliefs are opinions, not facts, and surely not truths and what we believe is subject to continual change and revision as we age, encounter new situations, and gain greater experience during our lifetimes.

Many religious beliefs are based upon fear of the unknown and around the conditions of our mortal existence. Beliefs are generally not scientific nor rational. They are often answers that defy scientific fact and rationality at the same time. This lack of both scientific fact and rational basis actually strengthen the pull and attractions of most "beliefs".

On Religion

Every man, either to his terror or consolation, has some sense of religion.

James Harrington

Religion is one of the most meaningful and yet one of most destructive of human endeavors. It is a both a source of solace for billions of people on our planet as well as the source of untold misery for so many others.

Most religions by their very nature profess to have "found" a single truth and these single truths are usually exclusive to, and separate from, another religion's single truth. Many religions tend to promulgate their version of the truth and brand non-believers as deviant and sometimes almost unworthy of basic humanity.

The intolerance of so many religions, combined with the violence perpetrated in the name of some particular religions has always bothered me.

I believe that religious choice is an individual decision even though it is often determined more by ones geography and cultural roots then by any true act of self-choice.

I believe that each society's majority government should protect all religions, but that this protection should not allow any religion to exercise prejudice, oppression, nor violence to any other group.

I have always been disturbed by the heinous and violent acts that are committed in the name of religion and spiritual beliefs, both in contemporary times, and throughout human history. There will always be misguided, and misled, religious followers who will so believe in the righteousness of their beliefs, and in their god, that anyone not believing in their approach are viewed as somewhat subhuman.

In spite of all the bad people who have given religion a bad name, I still maintain an open mind toward spirituality, and its important place in the human psyche.

There is great strength in the basic human soul, and the continual quest for understandings about the meaning of life and all of its mysteries, has spanned a pantheon of spiritual beliefs over the course of human existence.

Each of us must choose or define our own spiritual path through this pantheon of spiritual beliefs.

On Hope

Neither should a ship rely on one small anchor, nor should life rest on a single hope.

We ought to stretch our legs and stretch our hopes only to that which is possible.

Epictetus

Some people are perpetually hopeful. Others are perpetually in a state of resigned hopelessness.

I believe in continual realism-----knowing when the half-full glass is likely on its way down, or on its way up. Hope, like much of life, is attitude adjustment based upon continually shifting odds.

Perpetual hopefulness is dreaming. Its opposite is despondent pessimism. Neither is healthy or likely to create a happy climate.

You must know when to drop the hope and cut your losses, and when to double down and stick with a half full glass in realistic hope that it will soon fill up.

It takes knowledge, instinct, perception and realism to master the hope game.

Moreover, like everything else, mastering hope requires an appropriate attitude.

On Myths

Myths are necessary as ways of bridging the gap between our biological and our personal selves. Myths are essential to the process of keeping our souls alive and bringing us new meaning in a difficult and meaningless world.

Rollo May

Myths are not lies. They are imaginative patterns, networks of powerful symbols that suggest particular ways of interpreting the world. They shape its meaning.

Mary Midgley

Myths are an essential human need. People in traditional societies have a robust myth-history that provides guidance and meaning to their lives, enables them to endure hardships, and provides a basis for the orderly functioning of their societies.

Myths are not the same as the Mythology that we studied in school that connotates Roman, Greek, Norse and other cultural gods, although there are some historical contributions to our current myths from these sources.

Myths are all around us and form a mythosphere that is constantly with us, in our heads and in our culture. They are beliefs and traditions from our culture, stories from history and religion, images, and the symbols that surround us daily.

People in modern, westernized societies believe that those traditional myth-histories are akin to pagan rites, that they are merely ancient superstitions. There is a persistent belief that to shake them off and to denigrate them is the route to achieving freedom. The debunkers consider that any people that cling to traditional myths are backward and unenlightened.

> When men have looked for something solid on which to base their lives, they have chosen, not the facts in which the world abounds, but the myths of an immemorial imagination. Each of us has his private, unrecognized, rudimentary, yet secretly potent pantheon of dreams.
>
> Joseph Campbell

Yet modern, westernized societies create their own myth-histories because the need to believe and find meaning is an essential human need. In modern society our media along with psyche-social leaders create mythologies to explain the world.

We all need myth anchors in our lives. When society does not provide them we, or others around us, will invent them. Some thinkers like Rollo believe that myths are essential to mental health and that, "The very birth and proliferation of psychotherapy in our contemporary age were called forth by the disintegration of our myths. Through its myths a health society gives its members relief from neurotic guilt and excessive anxiety"

Myths can also inspire a people to greatness.

It is through myths that men are lifted above their captivity in the ordinary, attain powerful visions of the future, and realize such visions.

Peter Berger

The myths in our heads must be understood and appreciated. They are a part of our psyche about who we are and how we view our place in the world around us. They are a prism through which we view our individual and cultural history and form the backdrop for our spiritual and social beliefs.

Economic Health

Home is where you keep your stuff while you are out buying more stuff.

George Carlin

On Money

Money is one of the most difficult subjects to deal with openly and honestly. We often cloak our true financial situations with ostentatiousness when living beyond our means or modesty when we are living beneath our means. Many of us are taught that money is not a subject to be discussed because it is not polite, even though we are also taught that we need to be fiscally responsible.

While a visit to a medical doctor for an injury or ill health is a good thing, a visit to a financial counselor is a bad thing, and if done it is to be done quietly and as discretely as possible.

We often know more about the intimate lives of our friends, and sometimes even coworkers, then we know about their financial particulars.

Money represents security, freedom, and will determine whether you will reach your aspirations. Many learn to live on very little and are happy with a limited, self-determined, sufficient amount. Others have an unquenchable appetite forever more and are never satisfied, nor often very happy no matter how much they accumulate.

Money is a subject in which, our viewpoint about,

and struggle with, will change over time. Because everyone's style in dealing with the subject can be so different it can be a great cause of friction for couples, families and friends. For couples and partners of any kind it is vitally important for them to recognize that mutual understanding and agreement is fundamental to shared happiness.

On Time

Our days are like identical suitcases; all the same size but some people can pack more into them than others.

P. L. Andarr

While physical exertion can be helpful to your health, the physical stress and pressure of a fast-paced life is not. Stress and anxiety are killers and the main component of this is the pressure of deadlines, the pressure of time.

At some point, I became determined to be the master of time, not ruled by time.

I have learned how to slow down, to decelerate, by doing one thing at a time. I try to concentrate on it. I try not to think about anything else until I finish it. Then move on to the next item.

I have begun to think more mindfully and consciously about what I need to concentrate on in any given day in order to finish "my work". My objective was to establish order, symmetry, sanity and balance to my work and leave at the end of each day with a feeling of accomplishment and purpose.

Another cause of much of the frustration, anxiety,

and dissatisfaction that we often have, is the simple fact that we have not faced up to the reality that we cannot always be in control.

Our lives, jobs and inevitable happiness are at the mercy of others.

Unless we are absolute dictators at the top of an organizational workplace or governing system, somebody else is in control of us. We all have varying degrees of influence and ability to get some degree of control over our existence, but most of that which affects us is under someone else's control.

The realization and acceptance of lack of control, rather than being a disheartening moment, can be a moment of complete liberation. A liberation from angst, dissatisfaction, helplessness and despair requires just saying, "Yes" and bowing to the inevitable.

On Wealth

We should enjoy good fortune while we have it,
like the fruits of autumn.

Epictetus

Our attitude toward our material possessions ...
can lead to an inability to feel contented. If that
happens then one will always remain in a state of
dissatisfaction, always wanting more. In a way,
one is then really poor, because the suffering of
wanting something and feeling the lack of it.
So even though one may have a lot of material
possessions, if one is mentally poor then one will
always feel lacking and will always want more.

14th Dali Lama

Most of us, even those who profess to resist and
not be affected by it, are unconscious members of the
Western consumption class. Even when we resist
the specific products being promoted most of us have
absorbed the culture of happiness in consumption into
our subconscious value system.

While it is not possible to completely divorce
ourselves from this environment and still function
within the Western world, we can achieve some
sense of control by being "mindful" of the constant
bombardment and of our own actions and activities on
a daily basis.

I believe it is critical to mindfulness to keep your values in balance. This means spiritually, morally, and with a keen sense of purpose. To the extent that we can be mindful of our automated responses and actions, we can then strive to not be encumbered and ruled by them.

The Western culture is a continuous indoctrination machine that promotes the acquisition and consumption of products and services most of which go beyond the basic human needs for survival, enrichment, and fulfillment.

Examine why you purchase what you do. Do you really need what you bought this week, or did you just think you did, bought on impulse, or did its acquisition impress you with your success.

Every expenditure of money is an expenditure of your life energy that you are exchanging for more stuff. The stuff you actually need in life is actually very limited and very simple. It is the stuff we think we want that ties us down, that makes us think we must have to be successful.

It is this striving to succeed through consumption of material stuff that drains our life energy.

There are also many examples in our lives of consequence costs that exceed the original costs of items and because of this we need to be especially cognizant of the cheapness of any item that requires considerable expense to operate. The most two noticeable examples are the free color printer you sometimes get with a computer purchase or the free kitten from your neighbor. Most of us know the subsequent expense of color ink cartridges and cat food.

We tend to equate success with making money, with promotions, with increasing rewards.

I was coming into my office early one morning before the regular office hours and I exchanged pleasantries about the weather with the overnight security guard. I glance down and noticed the "how to be successful at..." book on his desk. As I walked to my office, I thought about the fact that he envied me just as I was beginning to envy him. Having achieved the success he sought, I had begun to tire of being successful.

It is one of life's ironies how we humans can engage in this sort of juxtaposition thinking.

My high-income life had worn me down. When I began thinking about what I actually did with the money I earned and about what I truly needed to live I began to realize that I might be a lot happier being a nighttime security guard. I fantasized about forsaking the tension, anxiety and everything that accompanied being "successful".

I ran across some old notebooks of my mother's

that have made me marvel at the frugality of her generation. She was a teenager and then young adult during the depression and then war period that gripped this country from 1929 when she was 10 until 1945 when she was 26. During that time in her life getting by was hard and called for many sacrifices. She had to keep track of where every penny went. It was a habit that she continued her entire life.

Well into her 80's my mother lived solely on her monthly social security and a small state government pension. She never seemed to want for anything, and would occasionally splurge on little luxuries. In addition, to my astonishment she managed to save money every month, money that she diligently put in a passbook savings account at the end of every month. Her secret was in the little notebooks where month by month, item by item, she kept track of every expenditure. Every one. At the end of the month whatever she brought in over what she spent, she put in her savings account. Then at the end of the year, she would summarize her expenditures and income by category.

The result was even more astonishing. On her death at 84, I was stunned to discover that she had saved over $90,000 from her "retirement" income. At a time in her life when most people are trying to stretch their social security to just survive; my mother was saving money every month.

My mother serves as my inspiration on the subject of frugality.

I have thought a lot about my mother's frugality. She is my inspiration. When her savings came to me by inheritance, I did not squander it by buying a shiny new toy or taking an extravagant trip somewhere. I paid off every debt I had. Her frugality made me virtually debt free. I know she would have approved and is smiling on me now.

However, what was more important than the money was the example she set for me so dramatically in her notebooks in her precise little handwriting. Every time I see examples of people whining about how they have such a hard time in getting by I think about my mother. I remember one time when I was with her at the grocery store and she was looking at the shopping cart of a woman with young children. What she was looking at were the food stamps in her hand and the type of food she was buying for those children. It was a look of pure scorn. The food was junk and instead of milk, there was soda.

I have made the transition into an understanding that I can get off the spending treadmill and I found that I suddenly have a lot more money in my account at the end of the month. I came to the realization that if I was exchanging my life energy for every dollar I earned then I was exchanging more of myself for something that I needed less of.

Needs

Needs are the basics of life that we require in order to exist and can be extended to those items that we need to be civilized and successful.

The most elementary of human needs are the traditional requirements of food, clothing and shelter. We should probably add to these items like basic transportation, health care, education and the accompanying items like insurance, bank accounts, etc.

Wants

Wants are fancy or enhanced versions of the basic needs to which we add a variety of items that we "could" live without and when times get tough we can cut out.

Keeping our wants in check and in perspective are a key to financial responsibility and curtailment of indebtedness.

Desires

There is both positive and negative desire. Desire which has proper reasons is positive, whereas desire which has no proper reasons is negative and can lead to problems. Desire is the prime mover in achieving happiness now and in the future.

Sometimes your intelligence may oppose your immediate desire because it knows the long-term consequences.

If desire pushes you toward the extreme, then your intelligence has the responsibility to check that course and return you to the center.

14th Dali Lama

Waiting sharpens desire. In fact it helps us recognize where our real desires lie. It separates our passing enthusiasms from our true longings.

David Runcorn

Desires are cravings for something we don't have but deeply feel that we want. They can be positive, as when they motivate you toward useful achievements, or negative, in that they draw you towards objects or experiences that are best left unsought or unachieved.

Savings

Saving for the future is often seen as a quaint and barely practiced endeavor by most people in the western world. Our economy has become based so much upon spending and consumption when we want something we buy it, not when we can afford it. Easy credit has made most people live beyond their means even when the mountain of debt has almost reached the breaking point.

The best advice that I can give you if you are unable to save regularly then is to at least control spending and to think of a dollar unspent as a dollar saved.

A $0 credit card balance should be as equally gratifying as a positive savings account balance.

Saving is never easy, but having saved is most always satisfying. Start while you are young by having a designated amount withdrawn automatically from your paycheck. Eventually you will not notice the difference when you see your account grow.

On Work

If you want a place in the sun, you've got to put up with a few blisters.

                                         Abigail Van Buren

Nothing great and durable has ever been produced with ease. Labor is the parent of all the lasting monuments of the world, whether in verse or in stone, in poetry or in pyramids.

                                         Thomas Moore

Pleasure in the job puts perfection in the work.

                                         Aristotle

The dictionary is the only place where success comes before work.

                                         Arthur Brisbane

Whatever work you do, find the joy in it. Sometimes it requires imagination to surface the joy in onerous tasks, but very often, finding amusement can be a good substitute.

One summer I had a job as a general laborer at the Illinois State Fair when I was in my teens. One day I was put on the manure crew. This work involved filling garbage carts from the piles of manure and straw outside the horse barns in 90 degree plus weather.

This was as unpleasant a job as I have ever done, but my fellow workers and I found amusement in it. We didn't doddle at the piles, we attacked them with speed and determination to get them all picked up as quickly as possible. At the end of a hot day we were dirty, smelly and had an amusing time washing ourselves and our clothes off in the fairgrounds vehicle washing station while cleaning our carts. We also discovered an interesting phenomenon---the smell went away at some point. To this day, often when seeing and smelling horse droppings, I have a flashback to those days I spent on the manure crew.

Quality

A man who works with his hands is a laborer; a man who works with his hands and his brain is a craftsman; a man who works with his hands and his brain and his heart is an artist.

Louis Nizer

Laziness travels so slowly that poverty soon overtakes it.

Benjamin Franklin

First-rate men hire first-rate men; second-rate men hire third-rate men.

Leo Rosten

If a man is called a street sweeper, he should

> *sweep streets even as Michelangelo painted,*
> *or Beethoven composed music, or Shakespeare*
> *wrote poetry. He should sweep streets so well*
> *that all the hosts of heaven and earth will pause*
> *to say, "Here lived a great street sweeper who did*
> *his job well."*

> *Martin Luther King, Jr.*

Doing the best you can at all times in your work will pay off over time. Sure there are times when the quality of your work will not matter and to be sure there are often times when no one will notice.

But, when it does matter, and when someone is watching, it will matter. This is one of the keys to being successful and becoming highly regarded in your work.

Connectedness

My generation is imbued with a work ethic that has made many of us into over achieving workaholics. We not only give our work the extra effort, we tend to always take work home and have great difficulty disconnecting from our work. Cell phones and e-mail connectivity was eagerly embraced by us and it has been our biggest problem.

I have discovered that it is not worth the cost to your soul.

Disconnecting can be painful. Several years ago

while on a three-week vacation I not only left all my electronic devices behind and removed my watch, I also did not read one newspaper, watch television, nor listen to the radio.

I did not miss a thing.

Why this was especially remarkable is because I not only carry a blackberry and a cell phone 24/7 but I also read five newspapers every morning. I have been this way my entire life.

This news hiatus was another step that I had made in breaking free from my workaholic ties to my office. I continued this no news habit in subsequent cultural trips to China, Tibet, India, Germany, Egypt, Spain, Costa Rica, Jordan and Israel.

Balance

Plenty of people miss their share of happiness, not because they never found it, but because they didn't stop to enjoy it.

William Feather

There is more to life then increasing its speed.

Mohandas K. Gandhi

What I do today is important because I am exchanging a day of my life for it.

Hugh Mulligan

You don't get to choose how you're going to die.
Or when. You can only decide how you're going
to live. Now.

Joan Baez

We can become addicted to our jobs. We can relish our title, income and status and become continually concerned with maintaining our position. This commitment can become obsessive and be to the detriment of our family and personal life. It is an easy treadmill to fall into.

Balance is about maintaining a healthy separation between work and all other parts of your life. It takes time to learn this balance.

On Success

*Success means doing the best we can with what
we have. Success is in the doing, not the getting-
--in the trying, not the triumph.*

Wynn Davis

The concept of success has different definitions
for different people and for all of us; this is a concept
that is subject to perpetual revision as we age, as our
circumstances change, as our attitudes change. For
some success means money, position or power, perhaps
all three. For others success is mere survival or having
a satisfying personal or family life.

This is a quiz for which there are no right answers.
Success is whatever "you" think it is, not what someone
else thinks it is. Do not fall into the expectation trap of
others values. Judge your success by your goals, your
expectations, and your aspirations.

Success does not require that we come out on top;
it requires us to reach a level in life that we have sought
as a goal. It need not be the highest mountain. A nice
comfortable hill may be all it takes for us to be happy.

Success is what you say it is.

Risk

When some misfortune threatens, consider seriously and deliberately what is the very worst that could happen. Having looked at this possible misfortune in the face, give yourself sound reasons for thinking that after all it would not be such a terrible disaster.

Bertrand Russell

By embracing risk, you will accomplish more than you ever thought you could. In the process you will transform your life into an exciting adventure that will constantly challenge, reward and rejuvenate you.

Robert J. Kriegel

A ship in harbor is safe---but that is not what ships are for.

John A. Shedd

The achievement of successes and of rewards inherently always carries with it the risk of failure and the risk of loss. The greater reward you seek often entails a correspondingly greater risk. It seldom works any other way. Therefore if you seek success or rewards in any endeavor, your appetite for risk must be proportionate to your tolerance and acceptance of potential risk.

Blame

People are always blaming their circumstances for what they are. I do not believe in circumstance. The people who get on in this world are the people who get up and look for circumstances they want, and if they cannot find them, make them.

George Bernard Shaw

He who cannot dance puts the blame on the floor.

Hindi Proverb

When we attempt to blame others for our problems, failures and shortcomings we are making a cheap attempt at unloading our situation on others, to find a scapegoat. We are refusing to accept either our own responsibility for our situation, or accepting that some bad things that are the result of the occasional negative flow of life will happen to us or that such occurrences will happen to us and that we all must reconcile ourselves to having them sometimes.

Happy and secure people have no need to blame others when things sometimes go awry in their lives. They take responsibility for what happens in their lives, both the good and the bad, and continue to move on.

Only when we accept that life can be hard and unfair can we begin to grow, but we as Tom Hansel says in his book, *You Gotta Keep Dancin'*, "Pain is inevitable, but misery is optional".

Failure

> *Something good always comes out of a failure or a great mistake.*
>
> *Albert Einstein*

> *Most great people have attained their greatest success just one step beyond their greatest failure.*
>
> *Napoleon Hill*

Failure is a terrible word and one that we don't like being associated with for any reason. It denotes we are a loser.

It should not always be looked at negatively. All failures are not bad, they often help steer you in a better direction. They can cause us to rethink what, and how, we are doing something.

> *Experience is the name everyone gives to their mistakes.*
>
> *Oscar Wilde*

Luck

> *I'm a great believer in luck, and I find the harder I work the more I have of it.*

Thomas Jefferson

Luck is a matter of preparation meeting opportunity

Oprah Winfrey

Luck is a matter of being in the right place, at the right time, to be the recipient of the decision or outcome that you've may well have set the table to happen. It is often neither chance, but prepared opportunity.

While luck can be a random occurrence you will seldom hit the basket unless you shoot a few balls at the net. The more balls you shoot, the greater your chance at being lucky.

On Plans

No battle plan survives first contact with the enemy

Von Clausewitz

While not all of life is a battle, planning follows the Clausewitz quote. I once naively believed that if I made a good plan, worked the plan diligently, then all my goals would be realized.

But in the real world you quickly discover that things don't quite work the way you plan for-----other people's agendas, circumstances outside your control, external occurrences, the vagaries of luck, accidents, mistakes, and a variety of other factors affect your ability to plan your future. In addition, you change your mind, new people come into your life, or leave it, and your values change as you age, new opportunities present themselves, and an entire host of changes occurs as you work your life plan.

When you graduated from high school you and your friends all set off on your separate courses, sure of your chosen direction, and certain of what you would attain. If you think about all of these high school friends, how many of them are where they thought they would be?

Probably not very many I am sure.

Well that is the way life is...

Dreams

Rose-colored glasses are never made in bifocals.
Nobody wants to read the small print in dreams.

Ann Landers

You should never be afraid to do what your soul
yearns to do. There is a spark inside of you that draws
you to some distant place. Never lose that wind that
pushes you forward to your dream place, no matter how
often you must deter the dream, never, ever abandon it.
When we lose the power to pursue our dreams we lose
our very soul.

You see things and say, "Why?" But I dream
things that never were and I say, "Why not?"

George Bernard Shaw

Since it doesn't cost a dime to dream, you'll never
shortchange yourself when you stretch your
imagination.

Robert Schuller

A dream is not something that you wake up from,
but something that wakes you up.

Charlie Hedges

Faith

*Faith is believing in things when common sense
tells you not to.*

George Seaton

*To accomplish great things, we must not only act,
but also dream; not only plan, but also believe.*

Anatole France

Faith comes from the heart and can be deeply held
by you and by others. It should never be subjected to
ridicule nor debasement by anyone, no matter how
skeptical one's faith may seem to you.

For a person to change their mind about an object
of faith it must be a result of their own self-examination
and decision, not by any external force or pressure.

On Learning

Be careful to leave your (children) well instructed rather than rich, for the hopes of the instructed are better than the wealth of the ignorant.

Epictetus

The person who knows how will always have a job. But the person who knows why will be his boss.

Carl C. Wood

In a time of drastic change, it is the learners who inherit the future. The unlearned usually find themselves equipped to live in a world that no longer exists.

Eric Hoffer

To acquire knowledge, one must study; but to acquire wisdom, one must observe.

Marilyn Vos Savant

Reading is to the mind what exercise is to the body.

Joseph Addison

We have all heard the teaching that learning is a life-long process, but all too often we cease to heed the call of learning, or worse keep our learning to narrowly focused on our particular line of work, our current way of thinking, and a narrow focus.

To be well rounded to what is going on in the world you should ready at least one newspaper every day and at least one newsweekly from cover to cover. How else will you understand our changing world? I am a bit over the top in my reading. I read five newspapers every morning and 7 newsweeklies every week along with about 20 monthly magazines. It is something I have been doing for almost 40 years and while my head is full of a lot of useless and faded trivia, I am nonetheless aware of the world in all its shades and hues.

> *Learning never reaches a terminal point. We die inside, even though our bodies are still alive, when we stop learning. We also become bored and boring. The solution is constant renewal, or learning.*

> *Mortimer Adler*

On Simplicity

Besides the noble art of getting things done, there is the noble art of leaving things undone. The wisdom of life consists in the elimination of non-essentials.

Lin Yutang

The art of being wise is the art of knowing what to overlook.

William James

If you choose to live simply do it for your own sake. Do not be an arrogant or overbearing follower of simplicity, forever expounding about how you are better then others because you have adopted the simple approach to providing for your needs at little cost. This is self-absorption that makes you look silly.

Simplicity should be pursued for its own purpose if that is a choice you wish to make. Just do not overlook the fact that most people in this world live simply because the have to live that way because they are poor. If you want to live simply do not do it to impress others with your frugality. Do it quietly and for yourself for your own personal reasons.

In the last year of my working life I choose to live very simply for very specific purposes. The first reason was to discipline myself to the lowered income level that I would receive when I retired. The second reason was to use all the rest of the money I earned that year to help my children pay off their student loans and those inevitable other indebtednesses that are consumer society allows young people to incur. I wanted to give them a little boost in life rather then to just buy more stuff for myself. So in effect, I worked an additional year for my children and because it made me feel good to do it.

.

On Discipline

With self-discipline, all things are possible. Without it, even the simplest goal can seem like the impossible dream.

Theodore Roosevelt

Discipline means choices. Every time you say yes to a goal or objective, you say no to many more.

Sybil Stanton

Discipline is the ability to bear hardships and adverse circumstances when confronted with them. Unfortunately, most people want instant happiness, success and wealth. It doesn't quite work that way in real life.

A lack of self-discipline that enables you to avoid the impulse for instant gratifications is one of the major reasons that people fail to realize their dreams.

You need to learn discipline yourself, to develop patience, and to have the willingness to make mistakes in order to surmount obstacles that happen along the way to your goals.

Focus

> *Mental activity can ruin a day, interfere with sleep, and greatly diminish our chances of being happy. And all because we just don't have very good filters. Every time we have a thought, we act like a dog when the doorbell rings. We jump up as though it's some important visitor. But it almost never is.*
>
> Daniel Gottlieb

The ability to focus, to concentrate on a single task, becomes ever harder to achieve in an age of increased distractions. As I sit and write this passage I am cognizant of the cell phone in my pocket that could ring at any moment and the light on my Blackberry lying on the table is blinking to tell me that a new message or alert demands my attention.

To focus is to do one thing at a time, to concentrate on the one thing, to think it through, to ponder on it, and to reflect on it.

Determination

> *Persistent people begin their success where others end in failures.*
>
> Edward Eggleston

> *Our greatest glory is not in never failing but is rising every time we fail.*

Confucius

It is not because things are difficult that we do not dare. It is because we do not dare that things are difficult.

Seneca

Unless you are by nature just plain consistently lucky then determination is what will separate you from someone who achieves their goals and someone who does not.

Determination is the grit to keep going, to not let failure deter you, to not let obstacles stop you, to not let setbacks discourage you----it is about getting up off the mat and keeping yourself going no matter what life or circumstances throws at you.

Determination is never giving up while you have a realistic chance, or sometimes just an outside chance, of succeeding.

Perseverance

As a goose is not frightened by cackling nor a sheep by bleating, so let not the clamor of a senseless multitude alarm you.

Epictetus

Perseverance is not a long race; it is many short races one after another.

I have learned that success is to be measured not so much by the position that one has achieved in life as by the obstacles which he has overcome while trying to succeed.

Booker T. Washington

Perseverance is the companion to determination. It is the long view. It is seeing beyond the current struggles that require determination to see your way through. While determination will take you over the current hill, it is relentless perseverance that will take you over the next one, and the one after that.

Determination is about winning battles.

Perseverance is about winning the war.

My son Brian decided in the 7th grade that he wanted to play hockey. The only problem was that he had never been ice skating. So he joined a recreational hockey team and learned both.

Brian demonstrated that he had both perseverance, and determination. I was a very proud father.

Both Jamie and Brian has amply demonstrated their true grit on many other occasions, and it is a quality that has been crucial to their well-being.

On Freedom

If a man does not keep pace with his companions, perhaps it is because he hears a different drummer. Let him keep step to music he hears, however measured or far away.

Henry David Thoreau

Freedom is among the most desired of human impulses. While it means different things to different people, it is a fundamental human yearning, and is a part of the social DNA of Western peoples.

No two cultures will agree on exactly what freedom means to all people There is a heartfelt desire for it, one that often cannot be articulated by virtually a people----but people both know it when they have it, and sometimes more importantly, they know when it is missing from their lives.

Responsibility

It is the act of an ill instructed (person) to blame others for (their) own bad condition

Epictetus

Responsibility for your own actions regardless of the circumstances is usually the most mature approach to any situation. To continually search for someone else to blame for your own mistakes or for simple bad luck is a narcissistic way of dealing with the ups and downs of life.

Independence

We think that we want to be independent, of free will, able to set our own course in life, free of constraints. What I think we really want is not to have any dependency show. It is more of a self-image and source of pride then a real desire. I think most people would like to live a life of seeming independence with a financial trust fund that quietly fueled our independent lifestyle and an unseen support group that was there for us in our times of need.

To be truly independent is to be able to either succeed, or to fail, completely on our own. Most of us like the idea of the succeed part, but not the fail part. We are attitudinally dichotomous, but this is OK. It is a natural human trait.

Consistency is a goal not an end.

On Retirement

Retirement is a word full of loaded connotations and visions. No two people will hold the same feeling toward the word and what it means to them. To some it represents an end of something. To others it is a goal. To still others it represents a new beginning.

I am among those who see it as a transition from one chapter of life to another. I am approaching it as an opportunity to find new purpose in my life.

Having a purpose in our retirement years means having very specific goals that you have concluded are important to you and that you have decided you want to achieve.

I do not plan to have a retirement based upon simply self-absorbed leisure nor do I believe that ultimately most of my generation will either. Those who do so, quickly tire of endless rounds of golf and fishing trips or discover that aging knees can't play golf every day. There are realistic limits to even robust activities without a purpose.

Retirement is when you can say goodbye to the purposes and goals that drove you during your prime working years. You shed the persona along with all of the triumphs that persona represented, and also all of the mistakes as well.

Retirement with a purpose is a time to be shorn of old ideas, motives, and complete mental baggage that were so much a part of the old you.

It is a time to let go of the old you.

You will reach your retirement years with many unrealized hopes and dreams. Finding purpose can either rekindle some of those older hopes or dreams, or you can place them all in the past and develop completely new ones. Before you rekindle an old dream you need to honestly ask ourselves if you are doing it because you truly believe that now they can be realized, or are you doing it to rectify an old failure. If it involves an old failure you may not truly be starting fresh, but may in fact be setting ourselves up to fail yet again.

A new beginning can be a time for burying the old, or a rebirth, but you need to question ourselves very hard if you are just putting a new front on an old failure.

Retirement can be looked on as a time of renewal of the self to a new purpose with the added advantage of wisdom about what is really important to you.

Many of us stumble and muddle through our working years. We are alternately driven and pulled, pushed, prodded and shaped along the way. Most of us never had a clue what we were going to do next but somehow we suddenly made it to that plateau called retirement.

There is no simple formula for finding your retirement purpose. It is inside all of us and will take you some time to bring it out. You cannot just sit down one afternoon and decide it. It is a bit of a journey. In the end, you may not find anything but simple peaceful retirement. That by itself will not be bad

I started my quest by asking myself two simple questions:

1. "What would I <u>like to do</u> the most if I didn't have to work"?

2. "What do I <u>not want to do</u> if I don't have to work"?

I continued thinking about the two lists and editing for several years.

At some point in my deliberations I began determining if there are part-time jobs in my community, or other ways to make money doing what I want to do.

I asked myself if health adversity could negatively affect my ability to fulfill my yet want-to-do-purpose. I then thought about how I would handle those adversities.

If you discover your unique purpose, whatever that may be, it will emerge from your pondering. Do not hesitate to share your thoughts with others. Prepare for realistic critique from those who care about you. This is both healthy and can help reinforce you and give you a warning if you are being unrealistic.

I believe that if you follow this path and ask yourself these questions in a realistic manner that you will find your way. But, if you don't find your unique purpose, then so be it. Muddling through got you this far, so maybe your retirement purpose is an idle relaxation from a life well spent.

Is that so bad?

Civic Health

On Participation

While it is not necessary to be an active participant in the civic affairs of one's community you should at a minimum be a regular voter and a rather aware one at that.

It does not take much and there is little direct reward for participation, nor punishment for not participating, but you should always keep in mind that millions of people around the world cannot even comprehend the act of secret voting.

It is a precious right and not one that you should take lightly nor take for granted.

On Patriotism

Patriotism is more than love of country. It is cultural ethnocentrism and can either be a positive or negative thing.

I have felt patriotism many times in my life and I hope it has been for good reasons and not just those that you experience naturally by being a citizen of a country. I confess to having been embarrassed about my country and my countryman at some times in my life. Generally though I have come to appreciate my country more every time I leave her shores, and I have always felt a special comfort when I have returned home.

I will admit that I have liked many aspects of other countries and societies that I have experienced, but judged in their totality, I have found no other place on earth that I would prefer to be a citizen of then the United States.

If that makes me a patriot then I am a patriot.

On Politics

My entire life has been spent as a political participant. In my younger years and at a few points in my middle years I got paid for working on political campaigns. I worked for Illinois state government on four separate occasions and on each one I was a political appointee. I have been a partner in six separate political consulting firms and raised my family, sent my kids through college, bought my parents a house near me in their declining years, and paid for my daughters dream wedding in Florence on the proceeds from political campaigns.

Yet it is my last thought and bit of advice that I want to leave to my children, not because politics is not by its nature an honorable profession, it is just not one that I look back upon as a badge of honor. There have been times that I believed in political candidates and that I was proud to see them do some good things.

At some point I have lost interest in politics. It seems as if it has ceased to be a contest between political philosophies but a nasty and brutish exercise in public nastiness. I lost interest when I lost respect with the inherent phoniness of the elected leaders in my country and community.

My interest has been somewhat given a little

second chance as I conclude this manuscript. Although I remain skeptical and jaded about the chances for real change, I feel that we have a chance for an improvement with my state's new Governor, whom I know has the right beliefs and values to attempt a revival in the spirit of public affairs.

Another real reason for my somewhat loss of interest at this time is because I know too much about why people vote the way that they do. It was how I made my living for many years. To understand electoral behavior with any sort of moral compass is cause for concern about the long-term health of our civic culture.

Nonetheless I am proud that my children vote. Jamie became a precinct judge and I was immensely proud of that. There are not many young ones. I was proud when Brian put a presidential bumper sticker on his snowboard. Of course it was for Ralph Nader, whom I didn't really care for, but the important thing is civic participation.

Recommended Reading

Happiness

📖 ***The Art of Happiness: A Handbook for Living*** by the Dalai Lama

A look at the philosophy of happiness specifically and the conduct of life in general by a revered philosopher who has one foot in the timeless wisdoms of the ancients and the other foot in today's world.

📖 ***Choosing Happiness; Life and Soul Essentials*** by Stephanie Dowrick

The message of this book is that individuals control whether they are happy by their attitude, self-confidence, and in kindness to others.

📖 ***The Five Things We Cannot Change; and the Happiness we find in Embracing Them*** by David Richo

This is a great book for an understanding of the "Givens" in life.

📖 *Don't Sweat the Small* Stuff by Richard Carlson

A book about simple ways to keep little things from overwhelming you and taking over your lives. Offers fresh insights in how to keep the minutia of life from overtaking and obfuscating our perspective about what is really important.

📖 *Finding the Sweet Spot: The Natural Entrepreneur's Guide to Responsible, Sustainable, Joyful Work.* By Dave Pollard

Explains how environmentally sustainable, socially responsible, and personally joyful natural enterprises differ from most jobs, and it provides the framework for building our own natural enterprise.

📖 *The Progress Paradox* by Greg Easterbrook

A look at the phenomenon of why the pursuit of progress can often leave us feeling empty and unfulfilled.

Values

📖 ***Cowboy Values*** by James P.Owen

A perspective on basic values as inherited from our cowboy and rural ethic heritage.

📖 ***Values from the Front Porch: Remembering the Wisdom of our Grandmothers*** by Jane Middleton-Moz

Time honored values from a time gone by, but not yet lost.

Journeys

📖 ***Dark Star Safari*** by Paul Theroux

For an introduction to the contemporary darkness of much of Africa and the difficulties of travel in failed and nearly failed states.

📖 ***In the Footsteps of Marco Polo*** by Denis Belliveu and Francis O'Donell

This is one of the best contemporary travel books that takes the reader through the route originally taken by Marco Polo in the 13th Century. It

describes the difficulties of ad-hoc traveling through the cultures and governments of the central part of Asia in amazing detail and how some things simply have not changed that much in 700+ years.

📖 *Ghost Train to the Eastern Star* by Paul Theroux

A tour-de-force trip by train, ferry and bus through Asia that shows a world changed, and in some cases unchanged in the last forty years.

📖 *When a Crocodile Eats the Sun: A Memoir of Africa* by Peter Godwin

This book will give you a glimpse into what it is like to live in a once prosperous and happy society that descends into heart-wrenching decay. It tales a story that will make whatever day-to-day troubles and concerns that you have pale by comparison.

📖 *An Empire Wilderness: Travels into America's Future*. By Robert D. Kaplan

Describes how America is a country not in decline but in transition, slowly but inexorably shedding its identity as a monolithic nation-state and assuming a radically new one.

Stoicism

📖 *Enchiridion* by Epictetus

A brief manual on the conduct of life by the Roman Stoic philosopher who's teaching was a big influence on Marcus Aurelious.

📖 *Meditations* by Marcus Aurelious

This is one of the most important of the books in the Pantheon of Stoic Philosophy

Meaning

📖 *A History of Religious Ideas* by Mircea Eliade

To understand today's major religions by a philosopher with a respectful and comparative view of them. In six volumes.

Rationality

📖 *Predictably Irrational; The Hidden Forces that Shape Our Decisions* by Dan Ariely

This book uncovers the forces that move us into making the kind of decisions that we make in our day-to-day lives.

📖 *Sway: The Irresistible Pull of Irrational Behavior* by Ori Brafman.

Makes you rethink how you think and to see the rationality of irrational behavior. Shows how e are all susceptible to the sway of irrational behaviors, but that by better understanding the seductive pull of these forces, we'll be less likely to fall victim to them in the future.

📖 *Supersense: Why we believe in the Unbelievable* by Bruce M. Hood

Explores how beliefs in things beyond what is rational or natural is common to humans and appears very early in childhood.

📖 *The Logic of Life: The Rational Economics of an Irrational World* by Tim Harford

Presents an x-ray image of human life and demonstrates that under the surface of everyday insanity, hidden incentives are at work that guide human behavior.

📖 *The Overflowing Brain* by Torkel Klingberg

Addresses the limits and possibilities of the human brain which has not evolved since the stone age. It explains how we all suffer from information overload, distraction, memory loss and attention diversion regardless of our age.

📖 *Against the Machine: Being Human in the Age of the Electronic Mob* by Lee Siegel

Puts forth an argument that our ever-deepening immersion in life online doesn't just reshape the ordinary rhythms of our days; it also reshapes our minds and culture in ways in which we haven't yet reckoned.

Myths

📖 *The Myths We Live By* by Mary Midgeley

The author contends that myths are not lies, but are rather imaginative patterns that suggest particular ways of interpreting the world. They shape our intellectual and moral thinking and help us find our place in the world.

📖 *The Power of Myth* by Joseph Campbell

This is the classic book on myth in modern society. It will introduce you to the body of knowledge on how primordial myths live today in our modern psyche.

📖 *The Cry for Myth* by Rollo May

This book describes how people need the solace of myths to find meaning in their lives and that when traditional myths are lost that new ones will spring forth to occupy the void in our lives.

📖 *American Myth, American Reality* by James Oliver Robertson

Explores the American myths: the stories, metaphors, and images we use, consciously and unknowingly, to explain our world. Tells of the myths we have created, inherited, transformed in order to understand our society and ourselves.

📖 *The Presence of Myth* by Leszek Kolakowski

Shows that no matter how hard people strive for purely rational thought there always has been a reservoir of mythical ideas and images.

www.ingramcontent.com/pod-product-compliance
Lightning Source LLC
LaVergne TN
LVHW051520080426
835509LV00017B/2134